Getting Started in Fundraising

Getting Started in Fundraising

Michael Norton

Murray Culshaw

Sage Publications
New Delhi/Thousand Oaks/London

First published in 2000 by

Sage Publications India Pvt Ltd
M-32 Market, Greater Kailash, Part 1
New Delhi 110 048

Sage Publications Inc
2455 Teller Road
Thousand Oaks, California 91320

Sage Publications Ltd
6 Bonhill Street
London EC2A 4PU

Seventh Printing 2008

Published by Tejeshwar Singh for Sage Publications India Pvt Ltd, laser typeset by Murray Culshaw Advisory Services, Bangalore and printed at Chaman Enterprises, Delhi.

Library of Congress Cataloging-in-Publication Data

Norton, Michael, 1942–
    Getting started in fundraising/Michael Norton, Murray Culshaw.
        p. cm.
    Includes bibliographical references and indexes.
        1. Fund raising—India. 2. Fund raising. I. Culshaw, Murray, 1939– II. Title.
    HG177.5.I4 N67   361.7'068'1—dc21   2000   00-042217

ISBN: 0-7619-9443-2 (US-Pb) 81-7036-914-2 (India-Pb)

Sage Production Team: Arpita Das, N.K. Negi and Santosh Rawat

Contents

Who this book is for

This book is for anyone who is interested in getting started in fundraising or in improving their fundraising skills. This includes the Chief Executive of a voluntary organisation and other senior management, a communications officer who would like to move from informing people to encouraging their support, or a programme manager who would like to increase the amount of resources available so that the organisation can do more or better work.

This book has been written especially for those who are working in the voluntary sector in India. Since all the case studies are taken from India, the book will nonetheless be of practical help to voluntary organisations and NGOs in other southern countries. If you are working in another country, then you will need to make allowances for the particular culture and conditions prevailing in that country. You might want to do your own research to identify local examples of good practice, or to identify those organisations or sources of information in your own country that can help you.

All the financial information is expressed in Indian Rupees. At the time of writing, the exchange rate was approximately Rs 43 = US$1. This means that:

Rs   100 = $2.33
Rs   1,000 = $23.25
Rs   10,000 = $232.50
Rs 100,000 (one lakh) = $2,325
Rs 1,000,000 = $23,250

Acknowledgements

The authors wish to thank the following for their contributions to this book:

- All those organisations providing case study material for showing that fundraising is possible and being prepared to share their ideas and experience.
- The South Asian Fund Raising Group for letting us use information compiled as part of their documentation of fundraising in India, which was funded with a grant from the Centre for Innovation in Voluntary Action.
- Ms Shikha Ghildyal for allowing us to use her fundraising letter which was written as an exercise and won first prize at the South Asian Fundraising Group's annual conference in Hyderabad in 1997.

Why fundraise?

Introduction

The way that voluntary organisations are being funded is changing. This means that many are having to think about fundraising for the first time. Here are three factors you should take into account if you want to consider the idea of fundraising for your own organisation:

◆ **Raising money from local sources** is an important aspect of building a successful organisation. Many people now feel that being heavily funded by 'foreign sources' does not create a feeling of 'local ownership' of the project. This can diminish its importance in the eyes of the local community as your work can be seen as being imposed and funded from abroad. With economic development, there is an increasingly successful local business community, a new 'super-élite' of the very wealthy and an expanding middle class population with disposable income to spend, all of whom are potential contributors to social need and change.

◆ International donors, such as the British Government's Department for International Development (DFID), which is setting up a Civil Society Fund in India, are **decentralising their grants programmes** and empowering their local offices to make decisions on local grants. They want to deal directly with Southern voluntary organisations. Previously they were supporting development through bilateral government-to-government aid programmes or by funding Northern NGOs to work with Southern voluntary organisations as their project partners. This changing relationship means that you have to know what funding is available, make contact directly with the donor and do the asking.

◆ **Government funding to voluntary organisations is increasing**, as many governments recognise that they cannot do everything on their own, and that other delivery systems might be more efficient or more effective. In health, education, welfare and development, governments want to work in partnership with reputable voluntary organisations.

Some international organisations have already responded to these changes. PLAN International, for example, has set its country affiliates a target of raising 30% of their funding from local sources.

At the moment, many organisations are concentrating their fundraising efforts on those same foreign donors that have been funding them previously and on approaching embassies for local grants. Some are also beginning to see the importance of widening their stake in society and building a supporter base in their own country as well—we also see potential for raising money from a wider range of sources (including local people, local business and government at national, state or local level).

For voluntary organisations funding is very important—the more money you can raise, the more work you can do... and the more impact you can have. But if you are to succeed in fundraising, this requires:

A **new approach** to how you see your organisation and its work, which focuses on public communication about the needs you are addressing and the importance and effectiveness of what you are doing. This means getting away from the jargon of development, and learning how to touch people's hearts and minds (and pockets).

New skills in identifying potential donors and in finding ways of asking them effectively—and then in thanking them and in building a long-term relationship so that they continue to support you.

Touching people's hearts

The Kargil conflict in Kashmir in 1999 generated an enormous philanthropic response from people all over India in solidarity with the war-like situation and to provide relief and welfare for the victims and their families. An *India Today* article reported the following examples:

- The Naxalbari Tea Estate management donated Rs 50,000 and the estate's 950 workers donated a day's wages.
- Some 1,500 sex workers in Delhi collected Rs 15,000 from amongst themselves.
- A 6-year-old girl in West Bengal collected Rs 1,000 in loose change from fellow passengers on her way to and from school. An 8-year-old in Rajasthan raised Rs 9,000.
- Ninety-eight women in a Chennai old people's home went on a day's fast and donated the Rs 1,700 saved on food to the war effort.

The challenge for fundraisers is to touch people's hearts (and their pockets) in the same way for the war against poverty and disadvantage.

Fundraising is never easy—there is too little money to meet the demands of everyone who needs it, and most of the times you ask you will be refused. But fundraising becomes a lot easier if you **understand the fundraising process** and if you **learn who to approach** and **how to ask**.

Getting started is the first and most difficult step in fundraising. Like learning to swim or to ride a bicycle, fundraising becomes easier with experience. Once you have 25 supporters, it is a short step to increasing this to 100, and then to 250 and eventually perhaps to 1,000. But finding the first 25 is a real challenge, as you have no experience of asking, no idea as to why people might want to support you or how much they might be prepared to give, no promotional materials and no examples of success.

But fundraising is possible. There are many examples in India of voluntary organisations that have made a start in fundraising, and the number is increasing all the time. They have had the courage to take the first steps, the ingenuity to develop ways of asking effectively, and the persistence to succeed—and not give up at the first hurdle they encounter or when the first person they ask says 'No'. Here are some examples:

> *'For how much longer are we going to walk on borrowed crutches?'*
>
> Padmashree K.S. Gupta, Lok Kalyan Samiti Eye Hospital, Delhi

◆ **Lok Kalyan Samiti (LKS)**, an eye hospital in Delhi, now funds the whole of its operating costs through local fundraising, which it gets from direct mail appeals and by asking people to sponsor eye operations and free eye surgeries for people who cannot afford to pay. Its Founder, Padmashree K.S. Gupta, has also started the OEU Networking Trust, which helps 30 eye hospitals in India use similar fundraising techniques for raising money and achieving financial sustainability.

◆ **SICHREM**, a group working for human rights in Karnataka, raised Rs 60,000 in 1997–98 through advertisement space for donors in *Souvenir*, a booklet on human rights with a directory of useful contacts and information.

◆ **Oxfam India Society** started a direct mail fundraising programme in India in 1996, sending appeals through the post to middle income people. This programme proved successful enough, in terms of the money and supporters that they have been able to get, for them to continue with it. After three years they have persuaded 10,000 people to support them.

> *'Developing our own fundraising capability has strengthened our organisation and its work.'*
>
> Hema, Association of Persons with Disability, Bangalore

◆ **The Association of Persons with Disability** (APD), Bangalore raised Rs 1.2 million during 1997–98 through direct mail appeals and events, in support of its education and vocational skills training programmes.

In this book, we want to show you how to fundraise. But we want to concentrate particularly on helping you identify local fundraising opportunities, so that you can begin to build support in your own region and local community, and begin to shift the balance away from dependence on foreign funds. But we will also look at ways of accessing foreign funds in your own country. Our aim is to:

◆ Help you understand **the importance of fundraising**, and how it can contribute to a strong and successful organisation. This will enable you to develop **a rationale for your fundraising**, and get everyone in the organisation to agree with why you are fundraising and its importance in your long-term strategy and goals.

◆ Show you some **simple, practical techniques** you can use to get started.

◆ Give you **examples of success**, and how you can learn from your own and other people's experience.

◆ Make you feel **confident that you can do it**, and show you some of **the personal and communication skills** that you will need to succeed.

What this book contains

This chapter provides **an introduction** to the whole idea of fundraising. It looks at some of the reasons for wanting to fundraise, some fears you may have about asking for money, and suggests how you might develop a mission statement for your fundraising.

Chapter 2 covers some of the things you need to think about and sort out **before you actually start fundraising**. This includes legal and tax matters, so that you know what's permitted and how to get any tax advantages that are available. You should find out about what others are doing, as well as your own organisation's previous fundraising experience. You need to think about the public credibility of your organisation, if you are going to get others to support you. And, there are a number of ethical issues you will want to sort out before you get started.

Chapter 3 looks at **fundraising sources and techniques**—who are the donors, and how to succeed in raising money from them. There are sections on getting money from individuals, from companies, from a range of institutional sources and donor agencies, through fundraising events, through overseas contacts and from tourism, getting support in kind and using volunteers, and income generation.

Chapter 4 looks at **how to develop a fundraising strategy** and plan your fundraising, and then see what resources are available to you to implement your plan and decide who will do the work, and how to recruit and manage a fundraiser (if you decide to employ someone specially for this).

Chapter 5 shows you **how to write an effective proposal**. This covers the structure and content of the proposal, how to improve your skills and how to cost a project to present to donors.

Chapter 6 covers **communication and public relations**. To be successful in fundraising you need to be able to tell people about what you are doing and why your work is important, as well as your wish for funds. Being an effective communicator is really important. There are sections on how to write a fundraising proposal, using case studies, producing simple and effective promotional materials, managing donor relationships and what makes a good fundraiser.

At the end of the book, we give information on **useful organisations and networks** in India.

We have tried to be as practical as possible, and many of the points are illustrated with actual examples. There are also exercises and checklists to help you relate the advice in the book to the situation of your own organisation and what you need to do to get started.

This is not a comprehensive manual on fundraising—for that you should read *The WorldWide Fundraiser's Handbook* by Michael Norton, which has been written specially for Southern voluntary organisations and is published in association with the International Fund Raising Group. This book is a practical guide to getting started, and is aimed at medium-sized voluntary organisations (without the resources that say an Oxfam can draw on), which may either have some experience or no previous experience of fundraising.

Reasons for wanting to fundraise

There are many reasons for **wanting to fundraise** from local sources. Note the use of the word *want* and not *need*.

Getting Started in Fundraising is unlikely to solve any immediate funding problems you might have. Developing new sources of support can be a lengthy process. It may take two or three years for your organisation to begin to receive sums on a scale that makes a significant contribution to your budget. If you have immediate fundraising problems, then you should concentrate your efforts on doing better with your existing donors and supporters.

Developing your local fundraising is not just to raise more money, it should also be something you want to do as part of a wider vision that you have for your organisation and how it should be supported.

> '*If you think that fundraising is just about money, then you are missing half the point. Yes, fundraising is about money; but it is much more than that. It is about learning to communicate effectively with the public, developing a network of enthusiastic and committed supporters for your cause, and building a strong and successful organisation which is able to face the future with confidence.*'
>
> Per Stenbeck, Greenpeace, Sweden
> speaking at a South Asian Fund Raising Group conference

Fifteen reasons for wanting to fundraise

Here are 15 possible reasons for wanting to fundraise—you may have others that you would like to add to this list. Consider these, then use the checklist (on p. 9) to set out your own reasons for wanting to fundraise. This is a first step in developing and agreeing to a mission and strategy for getting started in fundraising.

1. To **increase the amount of resources** available for your work; to meet the running costs of your programme and to expand and develop the work of your organisation.

2. To **create 'free money'** to develop your organisation's own agenda on your own terms. To create some resources which are not tied to donor requirements and, which can be used for what you want to do and when you want to do it. You may also use the money to create a **reserve fund** or a 'corpus' to generate an income from interest received on the money, or to tide you through difficult times.

3. To **reduce dependency** and the impact of donor withdrawal. Being less dependent on major funding sources is important, as many donors have their own agenda, which will change as their policies change. Sometimes you will find your funding terminated or cutback without any recognition of your long-term needs. It **strengthens the organisation** if it is supported from several sources, and becomes less reliant on just one.

4. To **move away from being a foreign-funded organisation** and to begin to be seen as a local response to a local need, mobilising local resources to solve local problems. Foreign-funded development can be seen as a foreign solution to local problems, or people may come to feel that the only way to promote development is by accessing foreign sources.

5. To **create greater sustainability**. To create sustainable streams of income for a long term. You can do this by finding a committed group of supporters interested in contributing to your work, or by organising successful fundraising events, which can be repeated year after year, or by developing the income-generating potential of your work.

6. To **raise capital through a one-off appeal**—for example, to pay for a new building, such as a hospital or school. This will require a major fundraising effort to raise the amount you need. Many of the people who support your capital appeal or one-off appeal, will be happy to continue their support for further requirements.

7. To **develop community links**. To root the organisation and its work in the local community, by getting the support of local people, local companies and local government.

8. To **build a constituency** of support, so that the organisation has 'the power of popular support' behind it. This can be extremely important for campaigning organisations, for example, those working in fields of tribal rights, environment or child labour.

9. To **involve other actors as stakeholders and partners**, and to create greater accountability and new lines of accountability. Being accountable to an individual who lives locally, to show them that their money is being well spent, is very different from being accountable to an international agency headquartered thousands of kilometres away.

10. To develop **local pressure for the work you are doing** and the issues you are addressing. Development can all too easily become something that only foreigners do, and the issues addressed (such as gender or child labour or environmental concerns) something that concerns only foreigners. Having local supporters brings the issue into local consciousness and politics. And a case could be made that if this does not happen, then the problems will never truly be solved.

Corpus fundraising: The pros and cons

Many organisations would like to create a 'corpus fund' which they can invest in and earn interest and dividend income from, and this income can then be applied to the work of the organisation. There are two views about this as a fundraising strategy:

For:

- It provides a useful stream of income on a continuing and assured basis.

Against:

- It is harder to raise money as capital to invest, than to raise money for projects that will have a direct impact.

- Much more money has to be raised as capital to create a corpus, than if you spend each year what you raise as income.

- It is hard to maintain the real value of a corpus fund, which is continuously eroded by inflation, and at the same time have sufficient income available to contribute towards the costs of your work.

- Needs are often so desperate that you would rather spend the money immediately than put it in the bank.

- The more you spend on your actual work, the more it can build your reputation as a successful organisation. This in turn will increase your ability to attract funds. Money put into the bank is 'dead money'.

This is not to say that corpus funds are a bad idea. We would all like to have the security of a large capital sum; and if somebody offered us a large legacy, then we would rush to create a corpus. But you should think carefully about whether fundraising to create a corpus is right for you at the moment, and whether you can raise a sum that is large enough to have any significant impact on your annual expenditure budget.

11. To have the opportunity to **'sell' the organisation and its work**. This process of marketing the organisation to donors and trying to convince them to give their support can be extremely creative in helping you recognise the importance of what you are doing.

12. To **take forward creative ideas and innovations**. Many donors like to support things that are new or different and, which may have an impact on the way things are done. Innovative projects provide you with a particular opportunity to raise money.

13. To **raise the profile** of the organisation. Fundraising means public communication. Public communication leads to greater recognition of the value of what you are doing and the importance of your organisation.

14. Because **people want to give** and **you can give them the opportunity** to support something worthwhile. However poor a country, there is always wealth around—from the super-rich to the professional middle classes; and many (although by no means all) are concerned about social injustice and would like to help if asked (or persuaded). If you are dealing with a minority group (such as a Tibetan refugee community), then members of that group who can afford to, will want to help. Even the poor can give and some people say that the most generous donors are those who can least afford to give.

15. To **build a strong and successful organisation** that can face the future with confidence.

Developing a 'mission' for your fundraising

It is important to list out why you want to develop your fundraising, and for the organisation to agree to these reasons. This will provide a context for your fundraising and for judging its success.

Taking the reasons decided above, together with others you believe important, you can then:

◆ define **your priorities** for fundraising;

◆ develop this into a **'Mission Statement'** for your fundraising;

◆ persuade the leadership of your organisation to **agree** to this Mission Statement;

◆ and then begin to **plan how to take forward the fundraising**;

By sharing the vision, you can develop a consensus as to why your organisation needs to develop its fundraising. You will be able to get the leadership of your organisation committed to the idea of fundraising, which is important—also to resource and support the fundraising activity, which is crucial if you are to succeed.

TO DO   Your reasons for wanting to fundraise

What are your reasons for wanting to fundraise? Is it:

- ❏ To **increase the amount of resources** available for your work?

- ❏ To **create 'free resources'** to develop your organisation's own agenda on your own terms?

- ❏ To create a **reserve fund** or a 'corpus' to generate an income from the interest received on the money and to tide you through difficult times?

- ❏ To **reduce dependency** on one source of funding and the impact of donor withdrawal?

- ❏ To **move away from being a foreign-funded organisation**?

- ❏ To **create greater sustainability**?

- ❏ To **develop community links**?

- ❏ To **build a constituency** of support, so that the organisation has 'the power of popular support' behind it?

- ❏ To **raise a capital sum** through a one-off appeal?

- ❏ To **involve other stakeholders and partners** (including local people and local business), and to create greater accountability and new lines of accountability?

- ❏ To develop **local pressure for the work you are doing** and issues you are addressing?

- ❏ To give yourself the opportunity to **market the organisation and its work**?

- ❏ To **take forward creative ideas and innovations**?

- ❏ To **raise the public profile** of the organisation?

- ❏ To give **people the opportunity to give**?

- ❏ To have **the opportunity to build a strong and successful organisation** that can face the future with confidence?

Tick those reasons which you feel apply particularly to you, and add others of your own.

Which are the most important reasons for your organisation?

Of the reasons you have ticked, select three, which you feel are the most important.

Developing a Mission Statement for your fundraising.

Now use these three reasons to write a short statement (30 to 100 words), which sets out the reasons for developing your fundraising. This will form the 'Mission Statement' for your fundraising.

What are you going to do with this Mission Statement?

Develop a plan-of-action for getting it adopted as the starting point for your fundraising.

Examples of Mission Statements for fundraising

'Our reasons for fundraising are:

1. to progressively increase the resources available to us for our work, which would enable us to expand our operations in response to need;

2. to reduce our dependency on any one source of funding and at the same time to increase the proportion of our funds obtained from local sources; and

3. to build a strong and successful organisation to meet future challenges.'

Here the task is really to identify alternative and additional sources of support locally, which can be used to supplement present funding. This could include, beginning to build a supporter base, organising a successful fundraising event, or obtaining support from local business. The fundraising strategy will be set within the overall mission.

Another example of an effective Mission Statement could be

'Our fundraising mission is:

1.   to mobilise local resources to ensure the continuation and development of our projects;

2.   to reduce the need for fundraising by mobilising support in kind and by managing our income generation projects more effectively; and

3.   to enhance public recognition of our organisation, the importance of what we are doing and the effectiveness of our work.'

In this case there is an emphasis on linking local projects to local support, so that local people and local business are invited as donors and stakeholders to ensure that the projects continue and, if resources are sufficient, that they are expanded or developed. At the same time, the organisation recognises that money saved is money that does not need to be raised, and that improving the cost-effectiveness of the projects will not only reduce the need for funds, but make fundraising easier. There is also a desire to bring the work of the organisation to greater public attention, so that there is a general recognition of its importance.

Now draft your own Mission Statement for fundraising. Having drafted this, put forward a proposal to the Management Board that sets out your vision and includes your plans.

Some fears about fundraising

Don't make excuses; fundraising really is possible

When considering anything new and different, and especially the idea of fundraising, the first instinct of many people is to say *'No'*; *'It's just too difficult'*; *'We don't know how to do it'*; *'We don't like asking for money'*; *'We're not the sort of organisation that could ever be successful'*; *'There's nobody interested in doing it... and I don't have the time'*.

These are just some of the excuses for doing nothing. There are many reasons that you could come up with for not getting started. The more you think about these reasons, the more difficult fundraising seems. When considering the idea of fundraising, think about the positive aspects, rather than about the difficulties. **Fundraising is never easy, but it is always possible**. In this book we will show you how!

Some basic fears

You may lack any or all of these:

Previous experience

You have never asked for money except from an international donor; and neither has anybody else in the organisation.

When you first start fundraising, you have no experience. But you will quickly gain experience, and you can always ask for advice from people who have some experience.

Fundraising skills

Fundraising requires skills, both technical and personal and you may feel that you lack these.

Many of the skills are just common sense. Others you will have to acquire. Seek advice from people who have done it. Go on practical skills training courses (where these exist). Use a fundraising consultant—if you are a large organisation and can afford the price.

The time to do it

Fundraising will take time, and you are already overstretched; so how are you going to fit this additional task into an already busy workload?

You just have to build the fundraising work into your busy schedule. Try to find ways of delegating some of your existing work to make space in your diary. Allocate time for your fundraising work—and make sure you use it.

Confidence

Because you have never done it, you are not confident that you can fundraise successfully. Confidence is an important factor in successful fundraising.

You should have a confident, outgoing personality. Once you get started, you will begin to find that people respond to you. And when you start to be successful, your confidence will begin to grow.

Belief in the cause

You may also feel that nobody will give for your kind of work. That it is simply not something that anyone will want to support.

This is just not true. Any cause can attract support, if need can be shown and a good case can be made. You are working for the cause because you are committed to it. Others will also feel the same way. You just need to find them and persuade them.

Credibility and a track record of success

Your organisation may be successful in its work but have no track record of fundraising success. It makes it much easier to give if somebody else has already given. But you are starting from a position of having no donors other than rather remote international sources.

You have got to start from somewhere!

People to ask

You may think that there are no easy sources, or that nobody has the wealth to be able to give, that your town or region is poor and needs to look to the richer world for support.

This is just not true; successful fundraising can take place anywhere. Part of the process of learning to fundraise is to find out about possible sources and how best to tap them.

Getting started in fundraising

The following is a case study showing how the Association of Persons with Disability (APD) in Bangalore got started in fundraising. APD, as a small organisation, had no previous experience of systematic fundraising and no well-designed promotional leaflets. In short, APD was starting from scratch. What this case study shows is that it is possible for any organisation to get started in fundraising. If APD could do it... then so can you!

Some practical tips

- **Learn by doing** rather than by going on training courses. Training does have its uses though. Some courses will be extremely helpful, where the trainer has real fundraising skills and practical experience to share. And on the training course, you will meet others in the same position as you are and be able to discuss your problems and ideas.

- **Share experiences with other fundraisers.** Be eager to find out what others are doing and to learn from their successes and failures.

- **Make a positive decision to get started.** You must really want to do it, but first get the commitment of your organisation and its Management Board.

- **Get a budget.** There will be some initial costs. You will need promotional material (such as a leaflet and a report of your work and achievements). You will need money to pay for some of the fundraising activities you undertake, as you may not cover all your costs initially. Fundraising is an investment in your organisation's future. You will need to invest time as well as money. Your Board needs to understand this and allocate or arrange for the resources you need to succeed.

How APD got started

Association of Persons with Disability (APD), Bangalore was established in 1959 by a small group of persons with disabilities and their friends. The organisation soon grew out of the garage in which it had been started, and now runs a wide range of programmes.

Over the years, the group has continued to receive small donations from well-wishers; however, the programme expanded mainly due to grants from international voluntary agencies and hard-earned 'self-generated' income from sales of products produced in their own workshops by persons with disabilities. In early 1995, APD decided to embark on a more systematic approach to seeking public support.

How APD's fundraising developed

Early 1995: APD secured the services of a consultant to help prepare a strategy to start up public fundraising. The strategy, which was approved by the Board, included:

◆ building a database of friends and associates (including visitors and suppliers);

◆ reviewing the leaflets and promotional literature that were available;

◆ keeping local newspapers informed of developments;

And most importantly, a decision was taken to recruit two full-time staff to concentrate on the fundraising work, with the direct involvement and supervision of the Board Secretary.

THE
ASSOCIATION
OF PEOPLE WITH
DISABILITY

APD's logo

Mid-1995: An appeal was made to international donor agencies to support the newly constituted 'Communications and Fundraising Cell'. Support was obtained, thereby underwriting the initial costs of fundraising.

End 1995: An advertisement was placed for a person to head the Communication and Fundraising Cell, an assistant and a secretary. Staff were recruited—unfortunately the person recruited to head the Cell soon resigned, but the other two stayed on.

Interestingly, because of the advertisement, Ogilvy & Mather, the internationally respected advertising agency, offered to help develop the fundraising strategy and various communication materials. It was not immediately possible to take up the offer, but contact was maintained and by 1997, O&M had become really involved—designing a new logo for the organisation and providing help with appeals, the annual report, the newsletter and posters.

1995–96: During this year, the first appeal was made to 67 'friends and well-wishers'. The response was very encouraging. Rs 41,300 was received from 11 donors, (an average donation of Rs 3,750). APD has always kept good records of its appeals and response rates, an important aspect of monitoring that provides vital data for planning. Articles began to appear in local newspapers. Donations increased from Rs 294,000 in 1994–95 to Rs 342,000 in 1995–96.

1996–97: The first 'cold' direct mail was sent to 5,000 people and more donations-in-cash and in-kind were received. Records were also maintained for 'in-kind' donations. For example, the Oberoi Hotel contributed a mid-day meal for the trainees in the technical school between June and November, valued at Rs 5,000 per month; Ms Singal donated a 10 kg bag of rice to be used in the school's mid-day meal programme. Altogether the value of the donations-in-kind during the period April 1996 to March 1997 was Rs 302,615, a considerable addition to APD's resources.

During the year a scheme was introduced for sponsoring mid-day meals for the school. In March, six persons donated Rs 3,500 towards a 'Remembrance Day Endowment Fund', and for 19 other days donations of Rs 350 were received, covering the day's expenses. The total value of donations during 1996–97 grew to Rs 784,000—8% of APD's expenditure.

1997–98: There was a gradual build-up of cold mail appealing (to new people) and warm mail appealing (to persons who had previously donated). A newsletter and an annual report (with design help from O&M) was sent to all donors and well-wishers, now numbering more than 1,000 people. There was increasing newspaper coverage of APD's events and activities. The total value of donations during the year, Rs 1,200,000, represented 13% of the organisation's increasing overall expenditure.

Lessons learned by APD

The main lessons learned by APD were:

- **Leadership** of the fundraising effort has been a constant issue. Staff have 'appeared' when required, but it is not easy to find the right staff or to retain their services. Staff turnover in fundraising, as in the advertising industry, is a reality the world over.
- Fundraising is **hard work**—it is constant, never-ending and often disappointing.
- However unexpected, **offers of help** are always a pleasure.
- A **system** for recording donations, sending thank-you letters and answering enquiries from donors and the public is absolutely vital.

Before you get started

So you've decided that your organisation ought to be developing its fundraising. But before you actually get started, there are a number of things you need to do first:

◆ Check the **legal situation** to see whether and how you are allowed to fundraise, and what permissions you might need to obtain.

◆ Check the **tax situation** to see whether there are any tax benefits available to donors to encourage giving, and if so, then how to obtain them.

◆ **Find out as much as you can** about the state of fundraising in India, and what other voluntary organisations are doing to raise money.

◆ You should also try to see what **experience of fundraising**, if any, there is in your own organisation, and who might be interested in working with you to develop the fundraising.

In this Chapter, we consider all these points.

Legal and tax matters

Are you actually allowed to fundraise? The legal situation varies from country to country, and you need to find out about the situation in your own country:

Are voluntary organisations allowed to fundraise?

In Western Europe and North America, fundraising is an important part of national life. In Communist and former Communist countries, such as China, Vietnam and Central and Eastern Europe, there were no legal frameworks for the operation of non-governmental organisations, and these are now only slowly being developed. In most developing countries, voluntary organisations have largely relied on foreign support, and so have not bothered to fundraise—and many of them know little about the legal situation.

India, on the other hand, has a well-established voluntary sector, with laws governing the running of societies and trusts and the granting of charitable status. Voluntary organisations in India are allowed to fundraise. Foreign funding has to be kept and accounted for separately from locally generated funds under foreign currency rules.

Is special permission needed to collect from members of the public?

In many countries, fundraising by charities is regulated to protect the public, and special licences may be required to collect on the street or to go from house to house to ask for money. In India, you do not require any special permission to collect in public.

Is special permission needed to raise money from foreign donors?

Most countries allow voluntary organisations to raise money from any source. A voluntary organisation in India has to register or receive 'prior permission' under the Foreign Currency Registration Act (FCRA) in order to receive foreign funds, which have to be deposited in a special bank account and accounted for separately.

Are voluntary organisations allowed to generate money by selling things?

Voluntary organisations are not commercial organisations, but many try to raise money through some form of trading or income-generation activity. In Bangladesh, for example, many of the large voluntary organisations have substantial trading operations (an example being BRAC, which owns a garment factory making garments for export, a cold storage plant for potatoes, and a printing press).

In India, what you are allowed to do depends on the constitution that governs your organisation. Look and see whether you are allowed to generate income by selling goods or services, or expertise and consultancy, or publications. Take legal advice if necessary. If you are not allowed to but want to, then you may need to change your constitution. Again, taking good legal advice is advised.

And if you do trade, there is the requirement that you spend the income you generate for the charitable purposes of your organisation. If you accumulate the profits, you may find that you become liable to tax.

Does your organisation's constitution permit you to fundraise?

Does your constitution give you the power to fundraise? If it doesn't, you may need to amend your constitution first.

Are tax reliefs on charitable donations by companies and by individuals available in your country?

You need to familiarise yourself with the tax situation on donations to charity and when they apply. Are there tax reliefs on donations for charitable purposes?

In many countries, the government encourages charitable giving by offering tax reliefs on donations to charitable bodies (which include development organisations). These may reduce the cost of giving by anywhere between a fifth and a half, providing a considerable incentive to donors, and especially to companies. If tax reliefs on donations do exist, how much they are worth depends on tax levels and the proportion of the donation which qualifies for tax relief.

Is your organisation qualified to receive tax reliefs?

What procedures are required for receiving tax-deductible donations? Does your organisation need to register? And does anything need to be done now?

Tax benefits in India

In India, two main types of tax benefits are available

• Section 80G

Non-profit organisations working in specified areas (which are deemed to be charitable) can register with the income tax authority under this Section. This enables donors (whether individuals or companies) to claim relief on 50% of the amount donated. On a donation of Rs 10,000, for example, a sum of Rs 5,000 could thus be offset against tax. At a 40% tax rate, this would result in a saving of Rs 2,000 in the amount of tax payable. The beneficiary organisation is required to issue a certificate in a prescribed format to the donor to enable the donor to claim the tax deduction.

• Section 35AC

This is more recent, and allows contributions to be 100% tax exempted. It is applicable to specified projects rather than to registered organisations, and generally covers the use of money for research purposes, but is being widened. To benefit under this Section, the organisation will normally have to undertake the project itself. Approval has to be sought from the National Committee for Promotion of Social and Economic Welfare, which is based in Delhi. Approval, if given, will generally be given for a period of three years. Although difficult to obtain, evidence exists that this tax relief can make an enormous difference to an organisation's ability to fundraise.

What to do

If you are starting to fundraise, you should check whether either of these types of relief will be available, and then obtain the necessary registration and permissions. If you need further advice, then consult an expert (such as an accountant who knows about charity tax reliefs or the finance director of a large voluntary organisation. The Centre for Advancement of Philanthropy (CAP) which is based in Mumbai, provides advice on charity law and tax matters, and there are a number of other agencies which do this.

Finding out what others are doing

It is also important before starting out, to find out a little about the customs and practice in your country regarding charitable giving and about what other voluntary organisations are doing to raise money. Try to answer the following questions:

What is the cultural situation in your country?

• Local support networks and self-help

There are many ways in which people give in response to need.

At a village level, there may be both informal and formal ways of providing for those in need, as well as systems of mutual aid such as burial societies where small contributions on a regular basis can provide insurance against some large future expenditure.

When people move to cities, the family and community relationships may be much weaker, and these traditions of mutual aid may then decay and even cease to exist. At the same time, though, there will be welfare charities providing money and services to those in need in cities.

Example: A video produced by the Hyderabad-based Centre for Development Communication (CDC), shows a widow in debt about to have her land seized by the moneylender, and the community organising a collection to redeem her debt, save her land and help her move forward in life.

• Religion

Religion provides a strong focus in many societies for charitable giving, with money being donated by members of any particular religious community to the temple, mosque or church to support the religious institution and to help those in need.

Many religions promote the idea that a portion of one's income should be donated to charity, sometimes as much as 10%. Hindu temples have a strong tradition of accepting charitable gifts from believers. The religious calendar can also provide dates when

---

CASE STUDY Using religious networks—MESCO

NGOs promoted by a religious group (Hindu, Muslim, Christian, Jain, Parsee, Sikh, etc.) may have particular opportunities to raise money at points in the religious calendar and through religious networks.

Mysore Education Social and Cultural Organisation (MESCO) runs primary and nursery schools, provides vocational training and supports the education of poor students. It also provides financial assistance for medical treatment and makes emergency grants at times of crisis. It raises two-thirds of its annual expenditure through *zakaat* (which is an obligation on Muslims to give a proportion of their income to charity).

The *zakaat* appeal is distributed two to three weeks before Ramzaan. Some 60,000 appeal brochures are printed, 2,000 are mailed out to contacts, and the remainder are distributed by hand to personal contacts, or by using volunteers (beneficiaries of MESCO who are paid a remuneration) who stand outside mosques after Friday prayers, or are circulated with newspapers by friendly newspaper agents. The total raised each year from this appeal is around Rs 2.5 million.

charitable giving is auspicious. In the Christian calendar it is the season before Christmas. In Islam, the festivals of Eid are a time for giving.

Some communities may have particular traditions of charitable giving. In India, and especially in Mumbai, the Parsees are a successful business community with their own religion (Zoroastrianism). They are leaders in charitable giving and have created charities to help Parsees in need; but they have also set up some of India's leading foundations (such as the Tata trusts), and have been at the forefront of several initiatives to promote business giving (such as the National Foundation for India, the India Business-Community Partnership and the Confederation of Indian Industry).

Religion as an agent for social change

'Whatever is to be given should be given with faith: It should never be given without faith. It should be given in plenty, with modesty, with awe, with sympathy.'—Tattiriya, Upanishad

Giving has been institutionalised in almost every major civilisation. A historical understanding of giving points to its theological, ethical and socio-economic roots. The Vedic notion of *daana*, the Christian notion of charity, the Islamic doctrine of *zakaat* and the Greek idea of philanthropy and altruism point to the universal validity of giving as a primary socio-religious need. In almost all tribal cultures, the mutuality and reciprocity of aid form an important aspect of community living and of collective spirit. In societies with a pastoral economy or shifting cultivation, gift giving can be seen as an aspect of the redistribution of communal wealth.

The term *daana* occurs repeatedly in the *Rigveda* and other Vedic literature. In its broadest sense it means unilateral gift giving. It denotes not only monetary endowments and gifts to monks and Brahmins, but also alms to beggars or needy travellers, the construction of *vihaaras*, alms halls, rest-houses, wells and other works of public welfare. The importance of giving during the Vedic period is evident in a verse of the *Tattiriya Aaryanaka*: *'Everything rests on daana. Through it, those who hate become friends'*. Though during the Vedic period *daana* was more or less confined to the occasions of big sacrifices, patronised by chieftains or kings, in the post-Vedic period, it became a much more prevalent practice among the common people.

Though the basic teachings of almost all religious and ethical streams lays great emphasis on the act of giving, one can find the underplay of power relations in almost every tradition. While the act of giving is supposed to be a selfless one, almost all scriptures emphasise the moral obligations by saying that giving helps to gain more reward in the future either from an all-benevolent and omnipotent God or from the future course of events.

Sharing was institutionalised in traditional Indian society through the establishment of institutions of hospitality and learning. These institutions flourished all over India, from Kedarnath in the north to Thanjavur in the south.

Contemporary international aid incorporating both ethical and strategic considerations can be traced back to the Marshall Plan in the 1950s, which provided aid from America to help Europe rebuild after World War II.

• The role of the State

In some countries, the government plays a strong role in meeting health, education and welfare needs of its citizens. In others, the level of provision is much smaller and there may be a feeling that it is up to people, families and local communities to provide for themselves rather than rely on a corrupt, inefficient or unwilling State. In the United States, for example, there is widespread distrust of government, and people expect that provision should be made through community leadership and charitable giving. In Europe, on the other hand, there is a tradition of State provision, and an expectation by citizens (despite a dislike of paying taxes) that the State will provide.

In India, there are many and large budgets available for social welfare community development, such as the Jawahar Rozgar Yojana programme for rural development. Financial pressures and inefficiency often mean that the impact of State provision is far less than it might be. There is sometimes a taint of corruption, and many voluntary organisations feel that they should not be taking government money. Bunker Roy, a voluntary sector leader and Chairperson of Council for Advancement of People's Action and Rural Technology (CAPART) says that voluntary organisations ought to be accessing government funding, if they feel that they can use it effectively, and by using it, achieve their goals.

• Building on local tradition

Fundraising, if it is to be successful, should try to build on the existing traditions of giving, rather than import fundraising ideas from the United States or Britain, where the culture and expectations of citizens may be completely different.

Try to learn as much as you can about the different fundraising traditions and opportunities in your own country, and in the regions and with the communities with whom you are working.

What are other voluntary organisations doing?

The next step is to find out as much as you can about what other voluntary organisations are doing about fundraising, and this includes:

◆ **Leading voluntary organisations in the country**, who may be the first into fundraising. In India, for example, Child Relief and You (CRY), which was set up in 1979, has been a pioneer in fundraising, raising money through child and project sponsorship, from cultural events such as film premieres and art exhibitions, and from gifts of services and products in kind. HelpAge India and Oxfam India Society, both associates of international development organisations, have also been in the forefront of fundraising in India.

◆ **Your 'rivals'**—other voluntary organisations of a similar size and doing similar work as you. What are they doing to raise money? What techniques are they using? How much money are they raising?

To find out, you can do the following:

Make friends with people in these organisations and ask them.

Get hold of their **annual reports**, promotional literature and the material they use in their fundraising.

Find out about the **fundraising events** they organise, even participate in them yourself!

Study the information carefully to get some idea of what works and what works less. You will find that many fundraisers are happy to share their experience.

Information and networks

You also need to research what information exists, and what networks there are to provide you with training and support *(for useful contacts, see page 152).*

• Information and publications

Are there any good publications that give information on donor agencies, foundations, leading corporate givers and government grants? These can be invaluable to the fundraiser, showing what is, and what is not, available.

Information can go out of date very rapidly, so it is important that you use recently published editions. It is also important that the quality of information they contain is high. Some directories are incomplete as they list only those who have bothered to reply to a questionnaire sent through the post. Some recycle old information without checking it. Some are published without any idea of the reader's needs.

A good starting point for finding out is the 'national association of voluntary organisations', whose name will vary from country to country, but which acts as a focal point for liaison and information dissemination, and which may also have a library of useful publications. In India, one national agency is Voluntary Agencies Network India (VANI) B–52, Shivalik, New Delhi 110 017, which has produced a useful directory of donors.

Another possibility is a **leading bookshop** specialising in social issues and development publications. There are two useful organisations that distribute books to NGOs in India:

◆ **Books for Change**, a Bangalore-based development publishing initiative, has over 1,000 publications which it distributes on behalf of voluntary organisations in India, including some books on fundraising and communication and the practical skills of managing a voluntary organisation. Books for Change, 28 Castle Street, Ashok Nagar, Bangalore 560 025.

◆ The **Other India Bookstore** runs a similar mail order service with books from India and other Southern countries. The Other India Bookstore, above Mapusa Clinic, Mapusa, Goa 403 507.

There may also be practical 'how to' publications available giving information and advice on particular fundraising techniques. There will be many more published in the UK or the US. Of particular interest are the following:

♦ **Charities Aid Foundation** (CAF) is developing an information service on international giving, has a series of publications on the non-profit sector in different countries, and is beginning to develop an international network of offices to promote and provide information on charitable giving. There is a CAF office in India which has published guides to the Indian voluntary sector, *Dimensions of the Voluntary Sector* and *The Non-Profit Sector in India*. Charities Aid Foundation, 25 Navjeevan Vihar, New Delhi 110 017.

♦ **Directory of Social Change** (DSC) provides a range of practical guides on fundraising in the UK, including the *WorldWide Fundraisers Handbook* published in association with the International Fund Raising Group. Directory of Social Change, 24 Stephenson Way, London NW1 2DP, UK.

♦ **<amazon.com>** This is an Internet bookshop which has a wide range of US publications for non-profits, and which can be ordered by post and credit card. You can visit amazon.com on the Internet.

♦ **The Chronicle of Philanthropy** is a centre of information in the US on fundraising. *The Non-Profit Handbook* is an annual listing of books, periodicals, software, Internet sites and other essential resources on fundraising. The Chronicle of Philanthropy, 1255 Twenty-Third Street, N.W., Suite 700, Washington, DC 20037, USA.

• Business giving networks

At a national level, there may be one or more networks of businesses, such as a Federation of Chambers of Commerce or a Confederation of Industry, which acts as a forum for business. In India, there are the Confederation of Indian Industry, the Federation of Indian Chambers of Commerce and Industry (FICCI) and the Association of Chambers of Commerce (ASSOCHAM). These now play a promotional and coordinating role in encouraging business support for the community. They may publish reports, with examples and case studies and directories of member companies, and some offer awards for good practice. See the section on company giving in 'Who has the Money' for details.

At a local level, there will be a Chambers of Commerce with local business membership. These can provide a good starting point for exploring the potential of local business support. Rotary Clubs, Lions Clubs, Round Tables and other such networks will also be useful.

There may also be associations of foreign businesses, which bring together US companies or multinationals, for example—many of which will have active giving programmes.

International Fund Raising Group

The International Fund Raising Group (IFRG) was founded in 1981 as a forum for fundraisers from different countries to come together, exchange ideas and learn from one another. The annual International Fund Raising Workshop in the Netherlands attracts around 500 delegates from more than 30 countries each year.

There are now 10 regional Fund Raising Groups (South Asia; East Asia; South-East Asia; South America; Central America and the Caribbean; Central and Eastern Europe; and the Middle East), which run an annual fundraising workshop and offer some fundraising training. The **South Asian Fund Raising Group** covers Bangladesh, India, Nepal, Pakistan and Sri Lanka.

• South Asian Fund Raising Group, A–97 Defence Colony, New Delhi 110 024.

• International Fund Raising Group, 295 Kennington Road, London SE11 4QE, UK.

• Networks and training

One organisation that has been active in promoting and supporting the development of fundraising in Southern countries has been the International Fund Raising Group (IFRG). There are now a number of regional Fund Raising Groups in Asia, Africa and Central and South America *(see panel above)*, and these may also have country groups affiliated to them. These regional and country fundraising groups will organise occasional conferences and training, and provide a network for fundraisers to share information and ideas.

In India, another source of information and advice is Murray Culshaw Advisory Services (mcas). Murray Culshaw was Director of Oxfam India from 1989 to 1994,

---

Making the best use of training

If you are getting started in fundraising, you may wish to get trained in the practical skills, which you will need to become a better fundraiser. To make the best use of training, you should:

• Check that the course is **suitable for your needs**. Some fundraising training assumes a level of previous experience or is designed with the needs of larger organisations who have the funds to invest in large-scale direct-mail programmes, which may not be appropriate to you.

• Check that the course is **practical** and covers more than just theory, that it includes actual examples and experiences of fundraising.

If you do decide to go on a training course, then:

• Write up your **notes** as soon afterwards as possible, while the ideas are fresh in your mind.

• Develop an **action plan**, which sets out what actions you will take as a result of the ideas you developed during the training course.

• Review **progress** after six months, to see what you have been able to implement and what you have achieved—and what you have not yet done.

where he was instrumental in getting Oxfam to move into local fundraising in India. After leaving Oxfam, he set up his own consultancy and has since worked extensively with smaller voluntary organisations in Bangalore to help them develop a fundraising and communications strategy and to get started in fundraising. He has also organised a number of successful training events.

Your own organisation's fundraising experience and credibility

Finally, you need to find out as much as possible about your own organisation. There are a number of things you need to do before you actually start asking for money:

What is your organisation's past fundraising experience?

It may be that your organisation is already raising money or has tried some time ago to do so. Try to find out as much as you can about past fundraising experience. Talk to your Director, the Chairperson, anyone who you think might know. Ask them these questions:

• What **techniques** were used and how much was raised? When was this done?

• What **worked well**? What did not work? And why?

• Who have been your organisation's **main supporters**? And for how long have they been giving their support? Is their support likely to continue?

• Does your organisation have a **membership** list? Or a list of people who have subscribed to a newsletter or bought publications. You should note the difference between those who **receive** a publication and those who **purchase** a publication, those who are just on a list in order to **receive information** about your work and those who have **supported you**—by giving money to you or volunteering their time.

What are your organisation's fundraising needs?

Start thinking about and discussing your organisation's fundraising needs. How much money needs to be raised? And when? This year, or next year, or perhaps if you are thinking strategically, in three years' time?

Some organisations get propelled into fundraising because they are about to lose a significant grant, which they need to replace. If you need to raise large sums quickly, then you will probably need to find another funder to take over—another donor agency with similar aims who is interested in what you are doing. If you are developing local fundraising with little or no experience of raising money in this way, then it will all take a lot longer than you think. You are building a fundraising base for the future of your organisation—and this takes time. It is probably wise to think about raising only quite small amounts in the first year or two.

Who in your organisation is interested in fundraising?

Is your Board interested? And do they know why they want the organisation to get involved in fundraising? Is this part of their long-term strategy and vision for the organisation?

Is the Chief Executive interested? And will she or he play a part in helping raise funds. Many leading donors will only want to deal with the senior person in the organisation, and fundraising is much harder if there is no commitment from the head of the organisation.

Is anyone else interested? If a group of people are interested, then they can support you in developing your plans, and also act as a working group to discuss ideas and review performance. These people might be other members of staff, board members, volunteers or outsiders with an interest in what you are doing or who have specialist communication skills.

What contacts does your organisation have?

It is always useful to have contacts with business leaders (who control company charitable budgets), with politicians (who can be useful in helping you access government funds), with leading experts and academics, with donor agencies and other international bodies, with the very rich, and with the media and advertising agencies.

Who you know can be as important as **what you know** when it comes to fundraising. So begin to widen your contacts. Sit down with senior members of staff, ask the Board, talk to some key volunteers to see if they know anyone who could be useful.

If you have a good rapport with the chairperson of a leading business, then that could not only be a good starting point in asking for support, but also in getting access to other senior business people. If you have a good contact in an advertising agency or a promotions company, then you might discuss the idea of business sponsorship and ask for their suggestions.

What are your successes and achievements as an organisation?

What have been the successes and achievements of your organisation since it was founded—and more recently? You will be asking for money for your work, so it is always helpful to recognise how successful you have been—as this indicates how successful you might be in making good use of the money you raise. Donors are more likely to want to give to successful organisations, and to back leaders and innovators who will use their money creatively.

A simple exercise is to write down a number of recent successes that your organisation has achieved, and then discuss this list with the Director and other senior staff.

What press coverage has there been for your work?

Having a good media profile is important to successful fundraising as we shall see. You can photocopy any published article describing your work and attach this to letters you send out. You can extract comments from the article and use these as endorsements of your work. You can contact the journalist, who must have had an interest in your work at the time the article was written, and suggest that there is now something new to report.

It is also important to keep **letters of endorsement** from experts and famous people that commend your work to others.

Before starting on fundraising, purchase a box file to keep press coverage, letters of commendation and endorsements and other material which helps demonstrate your success as an organisation and the value of your work. Call this a **Credibility File.**

TO DO   Create a 'credibility file'

A credibility file is a box file into which you put:

- **Promotional literature** produced by your organisation.
- **Letters of endorsement** from experts and prominent people saying how valuable and important your work is.
- **Case studies** showing successes of your organisation.
- **Photographs,** which you can use to illustrate how your organisation works and how much it is achieving.
- **Extracts from evaluation reports** that confirm how effective and cost-effective your organisation is.
- **Letters from users and beneficiaries** showing how important your work is to them.
- **Press cuttings** about your organisation's work.
- **Facts and figures** about the need you are addressing and its importance, obtained from a variety of sources.

You can begin to use all this as a resource when writing promotional literature or communicating with potential donors.

Your task: Go out and buy a box file to use as a **credibility file**. It's empty; start filling it!

TO DO List your successes

◆ List **six successes** achieved by your organisation during **the last two years**.

◆ Discuss these with senior staff, to see what else they would like to include on the list.

What promotional literature and other information has your organisation produced?

In your communication with potential donors, you will need good promotional literature, especially an **annual report** or review of your work and an attractive **brochure or leaflet** that describes your work.

What promotional literature have you produced already? Is it clear, well written and nicely illustrated? Or will you need to create something completely new to support your fundraising?

CHECKLIST Things to do before you get started

❑ Investigate the **legal situation**: Are you allowed to fundraise? What permissions do you require?

❑ Refer to your **constitution**. Do you have the legal right to fundraise?

❑ Explore the **tax situation**. What reliefs are available to individual and company donors?

❑ Find out as much as possible about the **cultural and religious background** to fundraising in your country and amongst the communities you are working with.

❑ Find out what **other voluntary organisations** are doing, and get copies of their promotional literature and annual reports.

❑ Find out what **publications** are available, including directories of funding sources and practical 'how to' advice.

❑ Find out about **business networks**: Which networks will be useful to you and how they might help you.

❑ Find out about **fundraisers' networks** and what training is available.

❑ Find out as much as you can about your organisation's **past fundraising experience**.

❑ Discuss your organisation's **fundraising needs**.

❑ Find out who else in your organisation is **interested in fundraising**.

❑ Explore what **contacts** your organisation has.

❑ List six **successes and achievements** of your organisation over the past two years.

❑ Put together any **press coverage** on your organisation's work.

❑ Review your organisation's **promotional literature**.

❑ Purchase a box file to use as a **credibility file**.

Most voluntary organisations in India either have no promotional literature, or what they have is far too long, badly written, boring and badly produced. Such is the importance of having good explanatory literature, that we are devoting a whole section of this book to this subject. You will certainly need:

◆ a simple **leaflet** (perhaps 4 pages A5 illustrated with photographs and printed in at least two colours) that explains the work of your organisation;

◆ a more detailed **annual report** or review of your work; and

◆ simple **fact sheets** about the issues your organisation is addressing (such as child labour) or projects that your organisation is undertaking.

Ethics and accountability

There are a number of issues around fundraising which need to be resolved before you start:

◆ **Who will you take money from?** And are there people who you would not wish to be associated with?

◆ What is **your accountability** to the donors and supporters you propose to raise money from? And how is this different from more traditional funder relationships?

◆ What **messages and images** do you give about your beneficiaries and the communities you are working with when you invite people to support your work?

Who can you take money from?

It is important to decide right at the beginning whether there are sources of support you would not be prepared to accept money from. Here are some points to consider:

◆ Is the money from a **foreign source**? Some organisations wish to avoid having foreign donors, as they feel that this might compromise their agenda. A child labour organisation funded purely from Indian sources is likely to have more impact on Indian government policy than a similar organisation funded wholly or very largely by international donor agencies. There may also be a feeling that *'We can do it ourselves'*, and that somehow the acceptance of foreign money is an admission of weakness and dependency. For example, Bharat Gyan Vigyan Samiti, a leading organisation promoting literacy, will not take money from a foreign source for this reason. And Kala Raksha, which promotes handicrafts in Kutch, does not because it feels that it would become less sustainable.

◆ Has the money been **illegally gained**? Is it 'black money' earned on the cash economy or amassed by a criminal, and being given in untraceable, used bank-notes? Has it been gained as a result of some corrupt deal? Would you accept such money?

◆ Does the money come from a **'tainted source'**, which is completely at odds with what your organisation is striving to achieve. A peace or human rights group might be offered a donation by an armaments manufacturer whose equipment is being used to oppress innocent people. A cancer charity may be offered a donation by a tobacco manufacturer whose products cause the very problem the charity is trying to deal with. An agri-business producing genetically modified seeds and pesticides might wish to support an agricultural development programme, but the organisation promotes sustainable and organic practices in the local communities where it is working. An organisation working with the youth may be organising an event, which a brewery wants to sponsor, and thereby appear to be encouraging drinking among young people. And so on.

◆ Will the donation create important publicity for the donor which is **completely out of balance** with the size of the donation. A major company negotiating a contract to build a power station might be offering small donations for community projects in the area in order to improve its image with the government as well as to try to counter any protest from the local community. Is your organisation prepared to be part of such an arrangement?

◆ Will any **bad publicity** that the company obtains, rub off on the recipient? Would you accept support from Union Carbide (responsible for the Bhopal chemical disaster) or Bofors (which is involved in a corruption controversy over the supply of guns to the Indian army), for example? And there may be many occasions when the donor may be the subject of bad publicity for its employment practices (such as a lockout of workers or being in court for paying below the minimum wages), pollution and adverse environmental impact. Will the bad publicity attached to the donor rub off on your organisation, and thereby affect your own image and credibility?

These are all questions that need to be asked **before** you start asking for money. It is better to have a policy in place before you ask, than to be receiving donations, which turn out to be unwelcome and then may need to be returned.

Here are some pointers towards developing a policy on donations:

◆ You might decide not to accept any **large donations received anonymously** (if a donor is known to you but wishes to remain anonymous, it is another matter).

◆ You might draw up a **list of criteria** for those companies that you will not accept donations from. Manufacturers of arms, alcohol and tobacco, international drug companies, agri-business might all be categories of company that you would consider for this list. There needs to be a good reason for ruling out any particular category of company. Then there is a question of scale. What if a major company has a drinks business, which is only a very minor part of its activity? You need to be clear about this. Your policy might refer to *'a company with a significant part*

◆ *of its activity in...'*, rather than *'any manufacturer of...'*. The wording of your policy is important.

◆ You might **set a limit** for the amount of money you are prepared to accept from any one business, so as not to be seen to be too dependent on them or subject to influence by them.

Developing an ethical donations policy

It is important that all organisations prepare themselves to face certain policy and ethical issues, which may arise while building up a communications and fundraising programme. It is not possible to provide a general prescription for all organisations; each organisation must decide matters for itself. But here is a sample policy statement on seeking financial support:

Policy on donations drawn up by Programme for the Welfare of Human Beings

Programme for the Welfare of Human Beings (PWHB) will set the highest standards in its approaches to fundraising and in accountability to all donors. An over-riding guideline will be to ensure that the good name and reputation of the organisation is preserved and enhanced through PWHB's communications and fundraising programme.

1. Receipts will be issued for all amounts donated by cash, draft or cheque; and letters will be issued for all donations in kind. For donations in kind, a separate register will be maintained, which will also indicate the approximate value of the donation in rupees.

2. PWHB will accept donations in cash up to a maximum of Rs 5,000. If donations of more than Rs 5,000 are offered, it will be at the discretion of the Director to suggest to the donor a specific item, which could be purchased with the donor's support or donated. If more than Rs 50,000 is offered the decision as to whether or not to accept the amount in the form of a donated item will be taken by the Chairperson, in consultation with one other member of the Board and the Director.

3. PWHB will accept all donations offered, provided no unacceptable conditions are attached. What is 'unacceptable' will be determined by the Director for amounts below Rs 50,000. For amounts above Rs 50,000, the Chairperson, in consultation with one other member of the Board and the Director will take the decision.

4. PWHB will not seek event sponsorship, joint promotions, etc, with any company, which is:

   • In a labour dispute with its employees.

   • Known to be under investigation by government authorities.

   • Known to be involved in production and marketing of alcoholic beverages.

   • Believed to be seeking public acceptability for questionable products or practices.

Decisions on these matters to be taken by the Director in consultation with the Chairperson and the Board as appropriate.

Policy statement agreed by the Board of PWHB on 17 March 1999 and signed by the Chairperson.

◆ You might draw up categories of **socially inappropriate activity,** which you would not want your donors to be involved with. Polluting the environment is one possible category. Exploitative labour relations is another.

◆ You might want to consider **sponsorship arrangements** and cause-related marketing opportunities more carefully on a case-by-case basis. Here, the good name of your organisation is associated with a company or one of its products in a high-profile way.

From all of this, you will be able to draw up a **donations policy**, which you should get agreed by your Board.

Agreeing to a donations policy

There are two contrasting points of view about whether to have a formally agreed donations policy:

1. **Take money from anyone** who offers it. Because:

   • all money is laundered by the bank;

   • the needs of the beneficiaries are such that any money is welcome; and

   • taking money from a 'bad' company, at least gives an opportunity to dialogue.

2. **Have a policy** on who to take money from (or rather who not to take money from). This should be set out as a policy and agreed to by the Board. If you have such a policy, it is best:

   • that the criteria are objective and measurable; and

   • that the policy makes sense with respect to your organisation's objectives, and is not seen as a matter of personal prejudice or political bias.

If you do have a policy, you will need to decide how much of a company's total activity has to fall within the particular criterion for support from that company to be ruled out. Many large and multinational companies have a wide range of products and services. If you rule out cigarette distribution, and cigarette distribution only represents 5% of the total activity, then does this rule the company out? Remember too that some companies trade through subsidiary companies or brands that do not have the same name as the HQ company, and that the HQ company may only own and control a proportion of shares of the subsidiary.

◆ You will need **good information** to maintain an ethical donations policy.

◆ You will want to **publish the policy** for your supporters to see, and to guide everyone who is raising money for your organisation.

◆ You may also need to set in place **a procedure for returning donations,** which have been wrongfully solicited and received.

Stakeholding and accountability

A voluntary organisation should be accountable to:

◆ its **beneficiaries** and the community it is benefiting;

◆ the wider **local community** where it is operating;

◆ the **staff and volunteers** who are actually doing the work;

◆ **society** and the **country at large**; and

◆ its **funders**, where the grant will be offered subject to certain requirements for reporting back.

Widening the fundraising to include individual and corporate donors and supporters creates an additional accountability to these people. Their interests and concerns may be different from those of other stakeholders.

◆ Their interest is more likely to be focused on the changes that you are making in **people's lives**. They are likely to be less interested in statistics and overall impact, and more interested in case studies and actual examples of the benefit of your work.

◆ They will **not want to read** long written reports.

Taking support from people and from companies at your doorstep means that you have to put some additional effort into reporting back, recognising their interests in your work and the issues that concern them. Larger supporters will appreciate personal contact, the occasional telephone call and possibly a reception or a meeting to be

---

How advertising can present the wrong image

An ActionAid advertisement for child sponsorship invites donors to contribute £180 a year (about Rs 2,500) with the slogan: *'Does this child need 50 pence more than you?'* The request is for 50 pence a day (about Rs 35). The picture is of an African child waiting for help. This advertisement has been brilliantly successful in mobilising support. But it implies that:

● all African children are starving, reinforcing an unfair stereotype;

● you, the donor, can do something to help—which is true. But it also implies that...;

● nobody in Africa is doing anything about the problem—which is completely untrue.

Yet in its development work, ActionAid promotes empowerment and self-help. Fundraising has to be done sensitively if it is to support the ethos of the organisation and its development agenda.

kept informed. All supporters will appreciate lively, interesting reports sent to them on a regular basis. And this is part of building a donor base. A donor now can become your friend for life.

This accountability can also affect how you see your work. Taking money from an individual is very different from taking money from a large international donor. An individual is giving his or her own hard-earned income to you, they are trusting you to make good use of it and you owe them a duty to do just that. It provides an additional but very reasonable pressure on you to make sure that your work is excellent and that you are making real changes to people's lives.

Maintaining the dignity of the beneficiaries

The messages and images you present when asking for money can be a problem area. The fundraising messages that work best are often those that present images of helpless people just waiting for a donor to help the organisation solve the problem. For example:

◆ People with handicaps and disabilities are presented as victims needing charity, rather than as people with the ability to help themselves and their own agenda of basic human rights for disabled and handicapped people.

◆ Child sponsorship focuses on one child and invites a donor to become a 'foster parent' of that child in order to help provide for its health, education and welfare needs. The sponsor wants his or her money used to help make a difference in one child's life. The arrangement may require the child to be grateful, and to show its gratitude by writing letters and having photographs and reports about its progress sent each year to its sponsor.

◆ Disasters such as earthquakes (remember Latur) and famines show outsiders coming in with aid, but not what people are doing by themselves for themselves.

◆ Leprosy patients are presented as people with a tragic illness rather than as human beings with their own feelings and aspirations.

There are two reasons why this issue is important:

◆ It is important to **maintain the dignity of beneficiaries** whose only 'crime' may be poverty and disadvantage. How you present their needs to the outside world is part of your own accountability to them as beneficiaries of your work.

◆ Many voluntary organisations have an **advocacy role** alongside their basic service delivery role. They want people to understand problems, and society's attitudes to change. But the 'negative images' used in the fundraising can create stereotypes, which set back the advocacy agenda.

It is important for a voluntary organisation, starting to fundraise, to discuss and come to an agreement about how best to present its case.

EXERCISE   Who will you take money from?

Would you take money from:

❏ An extraction company, which is known as a major polluter?

❏ A cigarette manufacturer or distributor?

❏ A formula baby food manufacturer?

❏ A company where the Chief Executive Officer is facing criminal charges regarding the conduct of its business?

❏ A company that is in the middle of a lockout of its workers for paying 'poverty wages'?

❏ A company that produces poor quality or dangerous goods such as fireworks?

❏ A company where there is a pending court case or public concern about its working conditions and record on industrial accidents?

Who has the money?

Different sources of funds

There are all sorts of ways of **raising money** for your work. Here are some of the main sources you might consider:

◆ individual donors;

◆ fundraising events;

◆ corporate donors;

◆ trusts, foundations and other grant-making agencies;

◆ overseas non-resident communities;

◆ tourists and visitors;

◆ government sources; and

◆ international aid and foreign funding.

There are also some ways of **saving money**, which in turn reduces your need to fundraise. These include:

◆ gifts-in-kind, where products or services are donated; and

◆ using volunteers rather than paid staff.

And there are ways of **earning money**, which include:

◆ the sale of your expertise, including training, consultancy and information; and

◆ income-generation schemes, including sale of craft items, plants and greetings cards.

In this chapter, we include the following information:

1. **Background information** on each source of funding.

2. **Advice** on how to raise money from a source for those starting to fundraise.

3. **Examples** of voluntary organisations raising money.

4. **Some opportunities** that might emerge and what to do about them.

> *'I am utterly shameless, I have no hesitation in asking my friends and persons to who I am introduced, for donations for a cause I believe in. After all I am not asking for myself.'*
>
> Rtn GM Rao, Treasurer and volunteer fundraiser for the Bangalore Hospice

Individual donors

Who are the donors?

There is a wide range of potential donors for your cause—each with different characteristics, each having a different motivation, each preferring a different way of giving, and each having a different pathway by which they can be contacted. It is important as a fundraiser to be clear as to who you plan to approach and how you propose to attract their support. Potential donors include:

♦ The **less well off** as well as the **rich**.

♦ The **young** through to the **elderly**, and everyone in between.

♦ **Men** and **women**.

♦ Those who are **affected by the problem** or in some way involved with it.

♦ Those with a known **commitment or interest in the issue** (for example, supporters of children's rights might support a street children project) as well as those who are only mildly interested.

♦ The **general public**—everyone through to those with a particular perspective.

♦ **Professionals** such as lawyers or doctors or scientists or teachers.

♦ The **whole of the country** to those living in a **particular region** or **city** or **in the neighbourhood** where your programme is located.

♦ **Family and friends** of existing supporters.

♦ **Members of interest groups and social organisations**, such as members of a campaign organisation, members of a Rotary Club or a professional association, members of a political party or trade union, or young people at school or college. If you have access to the membership of such groups, you can try to raise money from them.

The more clearly you can specify who is likely to be interested in your cause, the more successful you will be in reaching them. To find out about your organisation's potential for attracting support you can:

◆ See **who is already supporting you**—perhaps by carrying out a market research to find out why they support you. If you have some supporters already, a simple questionnaire will provide answers to this question.

◆ **Test different audiences** to see what the response is. You will almost certainly find that a wider range of people want to support you than you thought and for different reasons from what you imagined. Go out and meet people; talk at meetings about your work; organise a reception and give a presentation to people who have expressed some interest.

Why people give

If you can understand why people want to give, then it will be easier to get their support. Here are some reasons:

◆ **Concern about the problem**. Giving provides someone with the opportunity to do something significant for something they believe in.

◆ **Duty**. Many religions suggest that it is a duty to support those in need or who are less fortunate. Many people feel a sense of social responsibility to do something.

◆ **Guilt**. Guilt encourages the donor to give in the hope that the problem (and you) will go away.

◆ **Personal experience of the problem** or need or personal interest. This is one of the most powerful motivators for giving.

◆ **Personal benefit** of some sort. Many people like the status or recognition that comes with giving when their generosity is publicised.

◆ **As a memorial**. People often give to commemorate someone who has died or to celebrate an anniversary or birthday. In such circumstances, it is possible to arrange that a gift be given annually on the same day each year.

◆ **They are asked**, and it is hard to refuse. The main reason for most people NOT giving is that they are never asked. Research demonstrates this again and again.

◆ They wish to **participate in a fun event**—such as a charity bike ride or a marathon race.

◆ **Peer pressure**, where people know that their friends are giving, or where friends and colleagues are asking them to give. If a senior business person is doing the asking, then other business people find it hard to refuse. The same is true when senior politicians are doing the asking or are involved in the project as a patron or in some other capacity.

◆ **Tax benefits** on gifts made for charitable purposes. Tax is not usually the prime motivation for giving, but can be an important factor in encouraging people to give and to give more generously. It can be specially important for companies.

Different ways of giving

There are not only different types of donors, but there are also different ways in which they can give. A donor can support you by:

◆ Giving a **one-off donation**. Incidental support is not so important to you, as the cost of getting it will often outweigh its value. What you want are donors who:

◆ **Continue to give you support** on a regular basis, perhaps through making some form of commitment, for example by becoming a member or pledging to give money every month or annually.

◆ **Child sponsorship**, where a regular donation is linked to the development of a child. And there are many variations on this approach that link the donation to the support of an individual or a specific piece of work.

◆ Giving a **major gift** in response to an appeal.

◆ **Sponsoring a project** or a programme, paying all of the costs of this.

◆ Leaving a **legacy** to you when they die.

◆ Making a **gift-in-kind**. This can be anything you need from office space to items to sell at a charity auction.

◆ **Purchasing a gift item** (such as Diwali or New Year cards) or promotional material (such as T-shirts or posters).

◆ Supporting a **charity fundraising event**. And there are many types of event which can be used to raise money successfully for charity.

◆ Participating in **lotteries and raffles**, by purchasing a chance to win a prize.

◆ Raising money from **family and friends**. People who support can be extremely successful in encouraging their family and friends to give.

◆ Encouraging **colleagues at the workplace** to give.

◆ Becoming **a member** on paying a regular subscription or joining a **supporters group**.

◆ Giving time as a **volunteer** to help in your work or in your fundraising programmes.

Getting in touch

To be successful, you need to do three things:

• **Identify likely people** who might be prepared to support you, then...

• **Create the right message** that is likely to appeal to them, and then...

• **Communicate that message**, directing it to the person you are targeting.

How much to ask for

This is one of the most important decisions you have to make.

If you ask for too much, you may find that people are unwilling to give. If you ask for too little, it is a wasted opportunity. You should take the following into account:

◆ People don't like to be seen as being **either mean or over-generous**. They like to do more or less what others are doing.

◆ Start with **what you need to raise** and how many people you think you can persuade to give. This will give you an approximate sort of figure, and you can then think about whether it seems reasonable, or whether you will need to find more people who are willing to give.

◆ If the appeal is extremely **urgent**, you will find that you can ask for much more. A chemical spill at Bhopal, an earthquake at Latur, floods in Uttar Pradesh, a cyclone in Andhra or Orissa. All need urgent action, and people recognise this.

Dividing your work into units

Save the Children, a Mumbai-based voluntary organisation, has got Jet Airways to ask its passengers to donate money in an envelope of **The Magic Box** as an in-flight collection programme. Passengers are asked to give:

- Rs 100 to provide a good nutritious meal to one child for one month.
- Rs 125 to provide education for one child for one month.
- Rs 150 to provide vocational training for one child for one month.
- Rs 200 to provide medicines and diagnostic services for one patient for one month.

It is usually better to have a wider spread of amounts (say Rs 100, Rs 150, Rs 250 and Rs 500) to allow for different levels of giving. You should try to make each level of support seem really attractive and of good value, but make the larger donations seem even more attractive to encourage people to lift their level of giving. Rs 100 is a good level to start at, as many passengers will have a Rs 100 banknote in their wallets.

Lok Kalyan Samiti is an eye hospital based in Delhi, and asks people to support a cataract operation at Rs 200 per operation. It suggests that people might like to support:

- 1 or 5 or 10 operations...
- with payment yearly or half-yearly or quarterly.

It is often quite a good idea to ask for small sums to be paid frequently. Rs 5 may not seem very much, but Rs 5 per day amounts to nearly Rs 2,000 per annum. If you can link a small payment with a really useful piece of work (Rs 200 to give someone back their sight is not much), then you will find that donors are very happy to give. Lok Kalyan Samiti (LKS) sends a photograph of the person whose cataract operation you have supported with details of the date of operation, in order to build a link between the support given and what it achieves.

- People are more generous than you think. So **do not ask for too little**. It's best to ask for a specific sum, rather than for *'a generous contribution'* when they won't know how much to give.

- People respond better if the amount being asked for is **linked** to something you will do. This is why child sponsorship works so well. People can see that their money is going to support a child and that it will make a difference.

- You can provide people with a **range of options**, with the requested donation pitched at different levels. People can then select how much to give and what to support.

- You can **divide the work into units** and ask people to select how many units they would like to support, such as an eye operation or a tree being planted.

How to ask

Remember that:

- A **face-to-face meeting** works better than...

- addressing **a group of people**, which works better than...

- a **telephone conversation**, which works better than...

- a **personal letter** from **someone known to the recipient**, which works better than...

- a **personal letter** from someone not known to the recipient, which works better than...

- a **circular letter**.

The **more personal** you make your approach, the better the chances of success.

People respond to:

- The **cause** that you are addressing, and the way you are addressing it.

- The **organisation** and its reputation.

- **You personally**, and the leadership of the organisation.

- The **beneficiaries**, and **real life examples** showing their need and the impact of your work on them.

Meeting someone is always better than not meeting them. Having a meeting at **your premises**, where they can see you and your work, and possibly meet some of the beneficiaries, will always work better than meeting at their office.

Finding supporters: Some simple ways of getting individuals to give

If you are starting out in fundraising, you are probably not even aware of who your supporters are, and you have no experience of asking. The first step is to find a few people who might be interested in helping you, and to work out ways of asking them for support.

You have to ask them for something. Thinking about what to ask for and how much to ask for can be a really good opportunity to begin to create a 'fundraising message'.

Finding a few supporters is a first step to finding more people to support you, which can be a first step in building up a supporter base. Here are some first steps to take:

1. **Ask all those who are already connected** with your organisation to give something towards its work. It is always better to start from the inside than to immediately ask outside the organisation. Tell people that you are launching an appeal for funds, and that you want to raise a small amount of money to get started from among your staff, volunteers, Board Members, (and from their friends, who they should be asked to ask), inquirers and visitors, and anyone else you can think of. If the people who know you are not willing to support you, why should outsiders?

2. **Ask everyone who has given to you to suggest some names of people** who might be interested in the work of the organisation and in supporting it (again in a small way). Then draft a letter which **they** will send to their friends, and follow up if possible with a telephone call or a personal request.

**THE ASSOCIATION OF
THE PHYSICALLY HANDICAPPED, Bangalore**

Dated : 5th Dec. 1996

AN OPPORTUNITY ... to support a very worthwhile cause

Asma Banu is studying Engineering today and so is Krishna Murthy. Both of them studied at *Shradhanjali Integrated School (SIS)* and went on to get merit seats at an Engineering College. These former students of SIS overcame financial and physical difficulties to come up in life. Both are severely disabled and come from economically weak families; *they are our inspiration to sustain our efforts at SIS.*

SIS founded in the year 1973, is located on The Association of The Physically Handicapped (APH) campus. APH, a voluntary organisation, promotes a wide range of activities to assist persons with disability to build self-confidence and self-reliance and create positive attitudes in families and society towards persons with disability. *SIS is one of the few schools in Bangalore which addresses the needs of children with disabilities. It has 200 students 80% of whom are disabled and 20% non-disabled, the focus being on children from economically weaker sections of society.* Most of the students at SIS have locomotor disabilities. Recently we have started accepting children with learning disabilities and also having speech, hearing and visual impairments. SIS has classes from nursery to the 7th standard and is recognized by the Department of Education, Govt. of Karnataka.

Sunitha 3rd Std.

SIS also provides Medical Rehabilitation with support from *APH's own Physiotherapy and Orthotic Units.* SIS provides mobility appliances and arranges corrective surgery where necessary.

Other services provided to the needy children are every day baths, periodic haircuts, supplementary nutrition, medical checkups, uniforms, books, mid-day meals, and transportation. *All these services are virtually free of cost with nominal contributions from parents of children to ensure their involvement.*

The curriculum allows for many extra activities such as games, picnics, science exhibitions, dramatics, etc. and along with special teaching methods it provides all-round qualitative education.

Hon. President : **N.S. Hema**   Hon. Gen. Sec. : **M.N.V. Urs**   Hon. Treasurer : **B. R. Shivashankar**

HENNUR ROAD, (LINGARAJAPURAM), ST. THOMAS TOWN P.O., BANGALORE - 560 084, INDIA.
PHONE: 080-5475165,   TELEFAX: 5470390,   TELEGRAM: 'ABLEHAND' BANGALORE

All donations to **APH** are exempted from Income Tax under **Sec. 80 G.**
APH is registered under the Mysore Societies Reg. Act vide No. S2179 dt. 20.5.1959, FCRA Reg. No. 094420100 dt. 01.02.1985

First letter appeal sent out by APH, Bangalore

YES, I would like to support a child with disabilities through APH

Name _____

Address _____

_____

_____

I enclose my donation, made payable to "The Association of The Physically Handicapped".

☐ Rs. 500/- for a mid-day meal and nutrition programme for atleast 120 children

☐ Rs. 2000/- cost of basic education for one child for one year.

☐ Rs. 3500/- Endowment fund for mid-day meal (designated one day a year)

☐ Rs. _____ (your own amount) towards general fund to provide support services

● Please send me ☐ copies of this appeal to pass on to friends
● Note that I have written the names and addresses of friends on the reverse who might be interested in supporting APH.
● **Kindly return to :** N.S. Hema, Hon. President, "The Association of The Physically Handicapped", No. 11, Hennur Road, Lingarajapuram, St. Thomas Town Post, Bangalore - 560 084.
● All donations to APH are exempted from Income Tax under Section 80G of the Income Tax Act 1961. APH is registered under the Mysore Societies Registration Act No.111 of 1904 No. S/2179.

Reply form sent out with first letter appeal by APH, Bangalore

These two steps are the start of building up a mailing list.

It helps if you can:

◆ **Frame an appeal** in a lively and persuasive way. If you are raising money to repair a roof or for medical treatment for a sick child, you can set out a target sum you need to raise and **suggest amounts** that people might like to give.

◆ **Link a particular size of gift to a specific amount of work**. 'It costs Rs ... to restore the sight to a glaucoma sufferer' or 'Rs ... to plant a tree and nurture it for six months'. That way people feel that they are contributing to a real need and having an impact on people's lives. The concept of child sponsorship, which has worked so well in the North could be applied equally to the South, as organisations such as Community Aid and Sponsorship Programme (CASP) and Deepalaya have found.

◆ **Produce appropriate literature**. A simple leaflet explaining the work of the organisation with lots of pictures and case studies of the people you are helping. This can be an A4 sheet of paper folded once or twice. See the chapter on 'Communicating the work of your organisation' for more on this.

Start keeping a mailing list

You should 'capture' the names of everyone who has made a donation on a computer database (or a card index, if that is not possible). This is your 'donor base' of supporters, many of whom will continue to give over many years. It is sometimes known as a 'warm list', as it is a list of people who know about you and have supported you. Your aim is to build this up from just a few names to many thousands of loyal and committed supporters who are happy to help you. In India, you will be surprised at the response you will get from your warm list and with people's generosity. Possibly 10–15% will give something, and this 'something', when put together will be quite substantial.

You can also include the names of people who have not given, but who have expressed an interest in your work and would like to be kept informed. These are your **moral supporters** or **well-wishers**.

You should also put on to this mailing list, selected government officials and others you want to keep in touch with and influence.

You should then write to these people regularly (we suggest twice a year to start with). This can be in the form of a short letter outlining the work you are doing, highlighting some of your successes, and showing examples of people who are giving you money for your work, and might be accompanied by a leaflet or a short case study showing how you have been able to make a difference.

Start small. Try to get a mailing list of 50 or 100 people in the first instance. Try to get at least half of these people to give something—however small. This is a start. Your job then is to get more people to give larger amounts, and persuade them to give regularly.

Once you have a mailing list of 100, it is much simpler to expand this to 200... and then to 500... and then to 1,000. You will find that you are slowly beginning to build up a successful membership scheme or direct mail fundraising programme. Even organisations like Oxfam started in Britain with just a few supporters, although they now have millions of donors worldwide. Once your list begins to develop, this will require proper management (to add new names, to update the information on each donor, to ensure that amendments are made when a change of address is notified to you, and to remove names of people who seem no longer interested). You must also make sure that you do not have the same person on the list twice. This can give the impression of being inefficient and wasteful.

Keeping information about your donors

On your donor base, you should keep a record of:

* name and address;
* phone number;
* how much they have given and when they last gave; as well as
* other information, such as:

    'Particularly interested in our girl child education programme' or

    'Recommended three friends all of whom gave something' or

    'A lawyer and would be prepared to help with legal advice'.

Get some publicity for your work

Try to get coverage in the local press. A feature about the work you are doing; a news item on some latest success you have achieved; a publicity stunt to draw attention to your work; a request for volunteers; a letter to the editor making a particular point. Try to ensure that all publicity has an address where anyone interested can write (or a telephone number, but make sure that there's someone there to answer the telephone when it rings).

Publicity is covered in more detail on page 131.

Find other people to write to

There may be a list of people that you can use. A club or association of some sort with members might let you include a letter and a leaflet in a mailing they are sending out, or give you permission to write to their members. You might be able to get your leaflet sent with a magazine or journal to subscribers. It is also possible to buy lists of names and addresses from direct mail agencies. All sorts of lists are available, from credit card holders to members of a professional association.

These people are not your supporters. They have little information about your work, and you don't really know whether they will be interested in supporting you. These are called **cold lists**, rather than the **warm lists** of past supporters and friends and contacts. You will need to find lists that you judge will have the sort of people who might like to support you. You will send a simple leaflet that explains your work, together with a short appeal letter asking them to give and possibly a reply envelope.

This sort of promotion is expensive. It costs Rs 3 for postage alone; then there is the cost of the leaflet, the letter and the envelope, as well as the cost of doing all the clerical work and administration. You will need to get a return of around 1.5% just to recover your costs. The actual return you receive from mailing a cold list is likely to vary from 0.7% to 1.5% in practice. Don't be put off by these small percentages. Even if you don't quite recover your costs on this first mailing, you will be adding names to your warm list, many of whom will continue to give over the years.

A large national organisation wishing to invest in developing its fundraising might get together 50,000 names to be mailed in this way. A small local organisation might think in terms of a 5,000 mailing and an investment of up to Rs 50,000 in the promotion.

The sort of bodies that you might approach for this purpose include businessmen's clubs such as Lions or Rotary (where you can ask to give a talk about your work) or trade and professional associations. You must make the letter and leaflet bright, easy to read and designed so that people would want to pick it up.

These people know little about you, so you need to explain what you are doing in a simple but exciting way. You, on the other hand, do know something about them—

they may be well-off, largely male, business people, for example, doctors or teachers. You can reflect this in how you write to them. Making the letter seem personal to them and relevant is important.

The Hindu Mission Hospital in Chennai uses a wide range of fundraising techniques to raise funds. One method they are using, is to write to everyone in the Chennai telephone directory. The letter is a one-side printed letter. Between 600 to 800 are addressed every day, which means about 16,000 a month. They are held for posting until the end of the month (so that they can arrive around the same time people get paid). The expense ratio (costs as a proportion of income received) is about 20%. It takes about four months to get through the telephone directory and then they start again!

Keep a record of visitors and enquiries

Whenever someone visits or telephones you, make a note of their name and address, ask them if they would like to receive information about your work and put them on your mailing list. Make sure that your reception staff are trained to do this, and that their manner is cheerful and inviting.

Make contact with your local community

Most organisations fail to take advantage of the fact that they are part of a local community, and that some local people might be interested in what is happening in their neighbourhood. Some may want to give time or money—if you ask them. If you have a project in a neighbourhood, then go around knocking on doors asking to leave a leaflet about your work. If people seem genuinely interested, then:

◆ Make a note of this and ask them if they would like to receive **an occasional newsletter** about your work.

◆ Think about having an **open day**, and asking local people to come and see you. Invite a celebrity to attend, as this will be a 'draw' for others. Make sure you give out literature about your work. A variation on this is exhibiting at a fair or *mela*.

◆ Think about having **a local person as a Board Member.** This is always good for any locally-based organisation, as it will provide a link with the local community.

Organise a house-to-house collection

Visiting people in their homes and talking to them about your work can be an extremely effective way of recruiting support. A personal approach remember, is time-consuming, and requires the right people to do the asking.

House-to-house fundraising is particularly good for gathering support in the neighbourhood where the project is based or in an area where the person who is asking is living, and especially when asking people who live in the same apartment, street or block. The more volunteers you have who are prepared to knock on doors, the more you will raise.

Volunteers need to be properly briefed about the work of your organisation, trained to ask effectively, armed with promotional literature and a formal letter of authorisation by you to do the fundraising (on headed writing paper and with their photograph, so that they can be identified).

CHECKLIST Who might support you?

Which of these do you think you ought to be targeting to ask for support?

- ❑ The very rich.
- ❑ The middle income group.
- ❑ Professional people (think what professions).
- ❑ More elderly and retired people.
- ❑ Younger people.
- ❑ The general public, that is anyone.
- ❑ Men rather than women.
- ❑ Women rather than men.
- ❑ People affected by the problem or in some way involved with it.
- ❑ People with a known commitment or interest in the issue. Think about who these might be and what channels exist to make contact with them.
- ❑ People living all over the country.
- ❑ People living in a particular region or city.
- ❑ People living in the neighbourhood where your project is located.
- ❑ Family and friends of existing supporters.

Some of the categories overlap, such as men living in your city. But tick all those that you think will be particularly interested to hear about your work, and then use this to create a plan for your appeal.

A number of short case studies follow illustrating different ways of appealing to individuals.

CASE STUDY   Child Sponsorship, the Lok Kalyan Samiti way

Lok Kalyan Samiti (LKS) is an NGO in Delhi that runs an eye hospital and provides assistance to the poor and needy. It has introduced a child-sponsorship scheme to help children in need. *'It is high time we did our bit to wipe off the pain and misery from their lives. And this is possible only with your help... by donating as little as Rs 100 per month per child, you can take care of a child's educational, nutritional, medical and other developmental needs, thus giving a whole new direction to his/her life'.* From every Rs 100 donated per month:

- Rs 40 goes for his/her education (schooling and extra coaching provided where necessary).
- Rs 20 goes for nutritional support (to ensure proper growth and development).
- Rs 20 goes for medical needs (including health check-ups).
- Rs 10 is put into a bank account opened for the child (to inculcate a habit of saving).
- Rs 10 goes for family development (community service and meeting basic family needs) and administrative costs.

'To make the life of a needy child meaningful, please fill in the enclosed coupon and mail it to us... thousands of them are waiting eagerly for your response.'

LKS promotes this sponsorship scheme by circulating a simple leaflet and reply coupon to its mailing list of supporters.

CASE STUDY   Child sponsorship and Deepalaya

Child sponsorship is one of the most powerful fundraising techniques, as organisations like Community Aid and Sponsorship Programme (CASP) and Deepalaya are finding. But you need to be happy with the idea of child sponsorship first, and you need to manage and develop the fundraising. Once you have managed to get started, the returns can become impressive, as the following figures show for Deepalaya:

Growth in Deepalaya sponsorship income:

1991–92	Rs	64,000
1992–93	Rs	571,000
1993–94	Rs	1,238,000
1994–95	Rs	1,351,000
1995–96	Rs	1,813,000

Child-sponsorship income as a proportion of total fundraising income for Deepalaya in 1995–96:

Sponsorship income	Rs	1,813,000 (79.5%)
General donations	Rs	260,000 (11.5%)
Special events	Rs	79,000 (00.4%)
Souvenir advertising (special events brochures)	Rs	129,000 (05.6%)

CASE STUDY Child sponsorship, the SAMPARC way

Social Action for Manpower Creation (SAMPARC) was established in Bhaje village near Pune to provide a home and care for orphans and street children. It runs a children's village with houses, each housing 10–12 children. SAMPARC asks for Rs 600 per child per year to sponsor a child's education, or Rs 4,000 to cover the complete costs of supporting the child (food, clothing, medical needs, education, etc.).

SAMPARC prepares an album, with each page giving details of one child, including their name, a photograph and a write-up, with room for a sponsor's name and address. The album is circulated to prospective sponsors, who are people known to the Trustees and who are met in person, making it harder for them to refuse.

Sponsors are thanked by letter, they receive progress reports from time-to-time on their child, and are invited to come to the children's village. Full sponsorship has been obtained for 67 out of 72 children in the village, raising a total of Rs 268,000.

CASE STUDY School fundraising by Paripurnata

Paripurnata is a half-way house for women leaving jail or a hospital for disturbed people, providing a temporary home, medical services and vocational training. As a fundraising event for the organisation, the Head Teacher of a school was contacted, through an employee of Paripurnata whose wife was a teacher at that school. The Head agreed to allow fundraising, and a representative of Paripurnata addressed the school at assembly about the work of Paripurnata and the appeal.

Students from classes VIII, IX and X were given donation forms just before the summer vacation and asked to raise money from their family and friends. Instructions were given on how the money should be collected and recorded. Prizes were offered as an incentive; a badge for students collecting Rs 50 or more, a badge and certificate for Rs 100 or more, and a memento for anyone collecting Rs 1,000 or more. 800 students took donation forms, and nearly 500 received a prize. A total of Rs 37,600 was raised from this event. However, there was no follow-up with this school, nor was the idea extended to other schools due to lack of personnel.

Important points to note are:

- **Personal contact** with the Head Teacher was important when trying to introduce the scheme.

- All the forms, and an explanatory leaflet about the organisation, were **prepared in advance**.

- Students have limited financial means and may not be able to collect large sums. In this case, the average collected was Rs 80. But the **large numbers** meant that a **significant sum** was collected.

- Offering awards provides an **incentive** and also sets **targets**. In this case the cost of the prizes was Rs 2,500.

- Fundraising in schools offers the chance to **educate young people** about a cause, as well as make direct contact with people in your local community. The collectors might even be invited to tour the home to see the work that their fundraising supported.

- **Follow-up** is important. It might have been possible for Paripurnata to have made this an annual collection, thereby ensuring a regular flow of funds, and to extend the scheme to other schools, thereby increasing the amount raised.

- The **cost** of organising and administering the fundraising needs to be built into the budget.

- **People** need to be taken on as volunteers or in a paid capacity to promote and run such schemes, and they need to be properly briefed.

CASE STUDY   Getting started in direct mail—Paripurnata

Paripurnata was looking at another idea of fundraising, and a consultant suggested direct mail. A list of 100 people was drawn up, based on friends and family of staff and the Board and visitors to the centre. A simple letter that outlined the work of the organisation, its plans and the need for funds was photocopied on to the organisation's writing paper and signed personally by the Secretary. No specific amount was requested. A total of Rs 70,000 was collected from 25 people who replied, including two donations of Rs 10,000 each. The total annual expenditure of Paripurnata is Rs 560,000.

Following the success of this, Paripurnata has now taken on a fundraiser with the initial costs paid for by Bread for the World.

- The 25% plus response, that they received is really good. Perhaps a higher rate might have been achieved either through direct personal contact, or by including a simple leaflet showing the organisation at work. Certainly, the 75 non-respondents could be followed up with a reminder letter giving them information on the success of the appeal or through a telephone call. Mailing your appeal to a **warm list** is an excellent starting point.

- The same results will not be achieved with a mailing to a **cold list**. Paripurnata is now planning a much larger mailing. With a cold list, a much smaller percentage of people will respond, and the average donation is likely to be lower. This means that the appeal needs to be more direct; suggesting an amount or amounts that the donor might like to give; linking the amount to a specific piece of work, such as sponsoring one woman's expenses for a month.

- Getting started in direct mail is the first hurdle. Once there are supporters and you have set up a mailing list, the process of building on this becomes easier. It is possible that Paripurnata could obtain a large proportion of its funds from direct mail.

- Fundraising costs. Direct mail with the cost of the promotional material and postage is expensive. You need to allow for these costs in your plans. You may only generate a small surplus in year one. But you now have a list of active supporters, many of whom will go on to support you for many years if you ask.

- The most surprising feature of this example is that so many people who know the organisation are prepared to give generously. How many people can you think of who might like to support your own organisation?

TO DO   Getting support from individuals

Think about the following and jot down some ideas to consider further:

1. Local support in the community where your project operates

- Does the local community know about the work you are doing?
- Would they be interested? What could you do to make them more interested?
- Do you think there are people who might be interested in helping you? As a donor? As a volunteer? Helping out in an emergency?
- How can you best tell local people about your work?
- What are the next steps you can take?

2. Membership and donors

- How many people support you already? Who are they? How did they come to support you? How much are they giving (on an average)?
- Are there ways of increasing the number of people supporting you? What can you do to achieve this?
- Are there other groups of people who might be interested in supporting you? If so, can you define them (middle class professionals, doctors, lawyers, etc.—the more precisely you can define them, the easier it will be to find ways of reaching them)? When defining a particular category, think about how you might reach them to ask them for support.
- What do you think they will be interested in supporting? How much will you ask them for?
- What else can you ask for (support-in-kind, professional advice, people to volunteer in some way, etc.)?
- Develop some ideas for how you might promote your work and your organisation to these people.

3. Mobilising the support of prominent individuals

- Which prominent people would you like to get involved in the work of your organisation as a supporter, Board Member or Patron? Think about the names of some of the people you would like to involve, how you would like to involve them and how you can reach them to ask them. You don't have to have the President of India as your Patron. These could include leading business people; sports stars; music and cultural personalities and stars; political leaders; religious leaders; and local people who are respected.

4. Further ideas

- What other ideas do you have?

EXERCISE What would you do if...

What would you do if...

Somebody calls or writes in to say that they are interested in what you are doing?

Answer:

- Send them an information pack about your organisation.
- Include with this a request for support.
- Make a note of the name and address, and add this to your mailing list.

What would you do if...

Somebody sends you a cheque for Rs 1,000 as an unsolicited donation?

Answer:

- Thank them immediately in writing (or perhaps by telephone).
- Include with the thank you letter an information pack about the organisation.
- Put them on the mailing list.
- Write to them after some time to say how well their money has been spent.
- Invite them to a reception for donors.

What would you do if...

You receive a letter with a small amount of money from a child asking you to spend it for the benefit of less privileged children in India? She explains that it is her birthday money.

Answer:

- Thank her of course.
- Issue a press release to get the story publicised on TV and in the press.
- Design a campaign with your young donor as a role model to encourage other young people to give.
- Approach schools and colleges with your campaign material. This is an opportunity, which a creative fundraiser should jump at.

What would you do if...

You need to raise money really quickly?

Answer:

- Set out a good case in writing for why you need the money, putting your need in a positive light rather than letting people see things as a crisis outside your control.
- Telephone all your larger existing supporters and explain the situation to them; they may be prepared to help.

Organising a fundraising event

Organising an event can be a wonderful way of raising money for a good cause. But whether you are planning to organise a film premiere, arrange a celebrity cricket match or celebrate your organisation's 50th anniversary with a gala dinner, you need to think not just about the fundraising potential of the event, but of the cost and effort involved in putting it on and the possible risk of losing money (rather than making money).

For every event that attracts hundreds or even thousands of new supporters and gives everyone a good time, there is another that collapses, is rained off, or where the sponsorship is withdrawn at the last moment. While there is money to be made from a well-run event, many absorb a great deal of energy and deliver only small returns. You need to think about your capacity to organise the event, the likelihood of getting the audience you expect and whether you will actually make money from the event.

A Bhangra Pop Nite in aid of Alert India, Mumbai

One advantage of an event is that it can put you in touch with people who might not give you a donation—they may be interested in the event rather than the cause. And by participating in the event (and helping raise money for your cause), they might come to hear about what you are doing, become interested and may then decide to support you.

So if you are organising an event, make sure that it is well run and plenty of people attend it. But also make sure that your work is well publicised and give people an opportunity to express their interest. Keep a note of everyone who attends; you can write to them subsequently with a leaflet or newsletter and a request for support.

If you are getting started in fundraising, then organising an event can be a really good idea. But make sure that it's the right event for you, and that you get lots of people to participate and lots of good publicity.

CASE STUDY   How to organise an event to make money

The Hyderabad Council of Human Welfare organised an **Evening of Magic** with well-known magician P.C. Sorcar.

Mr Sorcar agreed to charge Rs 35,000, which was 50% of his usual fee for an appearance. The appearance fee is often the major cost and can eat up all your income if you are not careful. Getting someone to appear free or for a very reduced fee can be an important contributor to a successful event.

800 tickets were printed:

100 @	Rs	50	total possible income	Rs	5,000
150 @	Rs	80	"	Rs	12,000
250 @	Rs	100	"	Rs	25,000
200 @	Rs	150	"	Rs	30,000
100 @	Rs	200	"	Rs	20,000
800 tickets in total			"	Rs	92,000

1. The success of an event depends on **selling** a good proportion of the tickets.

2. Total possible income is reduced by giving away **free tickets**. You obviously have to give away some tickets to important guests, for the family of the performer, and possibly for beneficiaries of the organisation (in this case, street children).

3. Giving away too many free tickets can make it very difficult to **make money** (which is the whole purpose of organising it in the first place) from the event. But if the tickets are not selling well, it is better to give them away and get people to come to the event than to have empty seats. If tickets are not selling well, you might make an arrangement with a local school or an old people's welfare organisation to bring along some people to see the show.

4. **Additional income** can be raised through:

   • Getting the event sponsored.

   • Selling advertisment space in the programme or commemorative brochure.

5. You need to draw up a **budget** for the event. Costs will include:

   • Fees for performers.

   • Expenses for performers (travel, accommodation, meals). These can get out of hand, so be quite strict as to what you are prepared to pay when agreeing to terms, and set this out in a formal letter or contract.

   • Printing the tickets (these could contain an advertising message to defray costs).

   • Any costs of selling the tickets (for example, you may offer a commission to people to sell tickets, or a discount for bulk purchase). One way of ensuring the success of the event is to get together an 'Event Committee', where members commit to sell an agreed number of tickets to their friends.

   • Stewards and other people needed on the day at the event.

   • Equipment hire, such as sound systems, lighting.

- Decoration of the stage or the hall, including flowers, banners and displays.

- Administration and support costs for running the event. This might include a fee to an Event Organiser.

- Sundry and contingency—a budget for the unexpected. You will usually need it!

6. Try to **keep all costs as low as possible**. Ask for discounts wherever you can—for example, on the venue hire charge. Get as much as possible donated. Use volunteers where you can—but make sure that they are well briefed about what they are expected to do and about the work of your organisation. But you want the event to look good and appear well organised, so it may be worth 'investing' in decorating the venue and having efficient and smartly turned out stewards.

Making a shopping list to raise money

You are looking to raise money by getting all the main costs of your event covered. The best way of doing this is to make a **shopping list** of all the different items of expense, and then to ask people to cover the costs of one item until you have got all your costs covered.

Make a list of all the items. Then put a figure next to each. This need not be the exact cost, and can include an allowance for administrative overheads and the costs of organising the event (a rough rule of thumb is to double up on the actual cost); and you can also increase the amount you are asking for those items that will be most attractive. For example, in the list below, a water tanker is an essential, and people will be thankful for it; banners can contain a *'sponsored by...'* notice; joy rides and horse/camel and ice creams are fun items. So you can push up the cost of these. Remember your objective is (a) to **cover the cost** of the event and (b) to **raise money** for your work.

While trying to get each of the items on the list paid for, you could also try to find an overall sponsor for the event who would be asked to pay for all the bigger items (the launch, the tent and miscellaneous) at say Rs 75,000 in return for being acknowledged as the event's sponsor.

List taken from an 8-day children's carnival organised by **CHILDLINE Hyderabad**

Item	Amount	Item	Amount
Tent	Rs 25,000	Sugar candy and ice creams	Rs 4,000
Video coverage	Rs 8,000	Electricity	Rs 5,000
Photographs	Rs 5,000	Water tanker	Rs 1,000
Banners and hoardings	Rs 10,000	Security	Rs 5,000
Conveyance (car/bus hire)	Rs 15,000	Stalls	Rs 10,000
Ocean park	Rs 7,000	Miscellaneous	Rs 10,000
Joy rides	Rs 8,000	Launch	Rs 40,000
Horse and camel	Rs 5,000		
Car	Rs 3,000	**Total**	**Rs 161,000**

CASE STUDY   The Leprosy Mission's concert

In 1997, the Leprosy Mission organised a concert at the Siri Fort in Delhi with Jagjit Singh, a well-known *ghazal* singer. Some key points from their experience:

- They paid a total of Rs 250,000 for the singer and musicians, including travel and hotel expenses. Despite the fact that this was at a reduced rate for charity, it represented approximately half the total outlay.

- Various departments had to be contacted for permission. The entertainment tax division for entertainment tax exemption; the licensing department for a licence to organise the event; the traffic police; the law and order police; and the fire department. Each department asked for complimentary tickets; no cash bribes were given, and the Leprosy Mission managed to negotiate down on the number of free tickets.

- The auditorium capacity was 2,200. 1,443 tickets were sold and 250 free passes given.

- The ticket prices were Rs 700 (405 sold); Rs 500 (630 sold); and Rs 300 (408 sold). This generated a total revenue of Rs 721,000. The Leprosy Mission had initially wanted to price the tickets at Rs 500, Rs 300 and Rs 200. It is just as well that they opted for the higher prices, as this made all the difference.

- Most tickets were sold through sponsors and other contacts. Indian Oil, who sponsored the concert, sold tickets through their petrol stations, and took tickets for their staff. Standard Chartered, the charity's bankers, purchased 300 tickets; and through contacts, AirTel agreed to purchase 300 tickets and Citibank 50 tickets. These arrangements provided a guarantee that there would be a reasonable audience and that the event would not lose money.

- 1,000 copies of a souvenir brochure were printed to give to concert-goers, and this generated an advertising revenue of Rs 75,000 at a cost of Rs 50,000.

- Because it was a large-scale event, it was decided to hire an event manager to make sure that all arrangements for the venue and permissions were in order (at a cost of Rs 25,000). Other costs included an announcer from Doordarshan as compere (at a cost of Rs 5,000) and 10 ushers for the evening, who were paid Rs 800 each.

What sort of event?

There is an enormous range of events you can organise. These include:

1. Events that raise money

- **Sporting events** and tournaments.

- **Musical and cultural events** (such as art exhibitions, film premieres and concerts).

- Dances, dinners, fashion shows, discos for young people and other **entertainments**.

- Events involving **schools**, where the young are asked to raise money for you.

- **Participation events**, with the participants collecting sponsorship money from friends and contacts for their participation (sponsored walks, jogs, cycle rides, fun runs and anything else that can be sponsored).

◆ Bridge tournaments, quiz evenings and other **'socials'** organised as charity events.

◆ Heritage walks or cultural evenings for **tourists**.

◆ Picnics and **outings for families**, to interesting locations.

◆ **Auction** of donated goods and 'promises auctions' (where a promise to do something useful or interesting is auctioned off).

◆ **Raffles**, lotteries, sweepstakes and competitions where there is an entry fee for participants and a chance of winning a prize.

2. Events that promote your work as well as raise money

Where an event promotes your organisation and its work as well as raising money for you, there is a double benefit. Sometimes, the nature of the event draws attention to your work (such as a sponsored city walk for an environmental campaign, or a streetchildren's festival), and sometimes there is a more direct benefit where you can market your organisation's products or services. For example:

◆ **Exhibitions, festivals, fairs and other events** where you can have a stand or a stall displaying your work. Raising money can come through obtaining sponsorship to cover the costs of exhibiting.

◆ **Conferences and seminars** on subjects of professional interest that link the business world and the development world.

◆ **Craft fairs** and sales of work or plants.

Some events can be organised to draw attention to an issue or a problem. The march organised by the Christian community in Bangalore in November 1998, when 100,000 people took to the streets in protest against government inaction against the rising tide of communal violence, was an example of an event organised for publicity or advocacy purposes. Although it is possible to raise money from such events, fundraising is not the prime purpose.

Sometimes you can create an event just to attract publicity for what you are doing. This is sometimes called a 'publicity stunt' or just a 'stunt'. Good examples are Mobility India, which had a wheelchair demonstration at Bangalore City Railway Station to make the point that people in wheelchairs could not access the trains, and Greenpeace, which flew a hot air balloon over the Taj Mahal immediately after the nuclear tests in 1998.

Deciding what to organise

One starting point is to examine your market. Who are the people who will come to the event—the people who are already in touch with you (your donors, your members, your volunteers, the readers of your newsletter) or the people you can reach through a particular type of promotion? What are the interests of these people? Are they old or young, active and energetic, particularly interested in your cause? What are you and your helpers interested in—and what contacts do you have (access to performers, for example)?

Another starting point is what you are doing and whether any event can be linked naturally to it. You also need to beware of inappropriate events—a gala dinner to support a hunger project, for example.

Sometimes you will want to start from the sponsorship end, and ask a potential sponsor what sponsorship money is available, what sort of event they might be interested in, and what needs to be done for them to decide to back it. An alternative starting point might be to think in terms of some of the different types of event and see whether any seems appropriate *(see above)*.

Most events are run on a one-off basis—although you will always want to re-run a successful event next year, thereby creating a regular source of income for your work. Some events take place over a period of time—for example a knockout cricket competition or a film festival. More complicated (and more risky) events should perhaps be left to when you have more experience.

Depending upon the nature of your plans, you may need some sort of licence (to run the event, to collect money in a public place, or to run a bar). Check the legal requirements with the local administrative authority before you start any detailed planning.

Management of events

The ability to run an event well is crucial. It will almost certainly take much longer and involve much more effort than you think. There are three main approaches to organising an event:

◆ **Do it yourself**. But you need to make sure that you have the time and the skills.

◆ **Get a professional** to do it. Specialist event organisers now exist in most cities, and you can find out about them by asking an advertising agency. You could try to get them to work for you at cost or even for free. If you cannot persuade them to do this, then you must be prepared to pay their costs—which could be a fixed fee or a proportion of the income (say 25%).

◆ **Find someone else** who is willing to do it. Or **recruit a group of volunteers** and give them the responsibility for the event. But you need to be sure that people will do what they promise and in a way that brings credit to your organisation.

All approaches have their drawbacks and their advantages.

Because running an event is time-consuming and risky, you need to be really clear why you are organising it. You need to set out your objectives for the event right at the start. This includes:

♦ The amount of **money** you hope to raise.

♦ The numbers and types of **people** who will be involved.

♦ The numbers of people who might **continue to be involved** in some way in your work. This is only likely to be a small proportion of those who participate, and will depend on the type of event and audience. But it is up to you to persuade them.

♦ **Publicity**. This includes the press and TV coverage you can get for your organisation, for its work and for the event.

It is no good hoping to raise money, then failing to do so, and then saying 'Well, we did get some useful publicity'. If your aim was to raise money, the fact that you didn't raise enough means failure.

Having decided to organise an event, there are three factors to consider:

♦ **How to make even more money from the event**. Think creatively about how you can increase the income. You might decide to do a brochure containing advertising, or have an auction of donated items, or leave an appeal envelope on people's chairs.

♦ **How to avoid risk**. If possible, get as much of the income committed or underwritten at the start. If you are organising a dinner, for example, having a dinner committee of 20 people each promising to take one or more tables for the evening and committing themselves to pay for this will guarantee the financial success of the evening. Or you could try to get company sponsorship to cover all or most of the costs.

♦ **It always takes twice as long** to organise an event as you think. So start planning early. For a big event, you will need to start planning at least a year ahead.

Getting started

The following are the main decisions you need to make:

♦ **Do you want to organise an event? And why do you want to?** Organising one event a year can bring the staff, Board and volunteers together and create a sense of solidarity for the organisation. It can also raise money, bring in new supporters and get publicity for the work of the organisation. So if you are starting to fundraise, you might decide to organise one event, and to do something quite modest initially which you feel you are capable of doing. But decide what you want out of the event; set yourself clear objectives.

♦ **What sort of event?** This is an important decision. What you decide will be affected by your ambitions, your audience, your skills and any opportunities that present themselves.

◆ **What do you need to do next?** A first step might be to get together a small working group or committee under the leadership of one person, and give them the responsibility for running the event. They will need to produce a plan, a schedule, and a budget. Responsibilities will need to be shared by the group (planning the event, getting sponsorship, selling tickets, publicity, dealing with legal matters and permissions, finance, etc.). The Chairperson will need to co-ordinate everything and make sure everyone does what they are responsible for satisfactorily and to schedule.

Here are some further practical tips:

◆ Use **professional designers** to help you with any publicity material. They can make this lively, and this in turn will attract more people.

◆ Make the event somehow **unusual or different**. Give it a catchy title.

◆ **Do not be shy of asking for money**. That's the purpose of having the event in the first place. Think of all the different ways in which you might get those who attend to support you.

◆ **Do not sell the tickets too cheaply**. If you are worried about value, it is better to concentrate on making the event **better** rather than making it **cheaper**.

◆ Make sure that everything is **well documented**. You can learn from your mistakes as well as from your successes. So...

◆ **Immediately after the event, organise a debriefing session**. You can then decide what you did right, what wrong. You can decide how you would organise it better when you do it again.

◆ If the event has been successful, **start planning the event for next year**. But do it even better next time, get even more people to attend, raise even more money, get even better publicity. Immediately after the event is a good time to get started on this.

Participation events

There are other types of events that have been used very successfully to raise money. This is where the participants collect money from their friends and colleagues to take part in some sort of challenge or fun event. For example:

◆ A **sponsored cycle ride**. This could be over a 50 km distance, where participants ask to be sponsored for a few rupees for each kilometre they complete. Child Relief and You (CRY) had two cyclists ride from Chennai to Delhi, stopping all along the way to give interviews and promote the work of CRY.

◆ A **sponsored run**. This could be a marathon or it could be a 'fun run', which would be much shorter and have some participants dressing in fancy costume. One variation of this is a relay marathon, where a team of, say eight people

EXERCISE   What would you do if...

What would you do if...

Someone telephones you to say that an entertainer is available, and would you like to use her for a fundraising concert.

Answer:

- Check whether the entertainer comes free or for a fee, and any other expenses that you will be obliged to pay. And check the standing of the entertainer. Is she popular? Will anyone want to see her?
- Think whether the event is right for you, and whether you have the capacity to organise such an event. If the answer is yes, then...
- Write a rough budget for the event, and get it approved, so that there is money available to hire a hall and equipment, print invitations and a poster, etc.
- Bring together a small planning team to take the idea forward.

What would you do if...

You are organising an event, scheduled for next week, and only 25% of the tickets have been sold.

Answer:

- Discuss the situation with a small group of people, including the event organiser, the accountant, and possibly the Chief Executive.
- Think about how to sell more tickets; particularly whether there are people who might buy a large number of tickets in bulk for distribution to employees or to enable children from a school for the handicapped to attend.
- Plan how to give free tickets to people who would like to come, but can't afford to buy the tickets, such as school children and pensioners. If you can't sell the tickets, remember, it is better to have people sitting in the seats than having them empty.
- At the last moment get an article in the newspaper that free tickets are available to the first 100 callers.

What would you do if...

You were invited to participate in a Social Development Fair in one of the metros.

Answer:

- Check with the people who participated last year, to see how it was run and whether it is worth participating in.
- Consider the costs and the benefits. Set some objectives for participating in the exhibition; what you hope to get out of it, whether it is a sensible use of your time and money, and why should you do it.
- If you do think it's worthwhile, then set up a small planning group with different responsibilities; display, organising an event of some sort to bring people to see you, PR, fundraising (to get the cost sponsored).

complete a marathon (each running about 5 km), and this is often attractive to businesses who put up their team to compete with teams from other businesses.

♦ Something more **thrilling** or **challenging**, such as parachuting or rope climbing down a tower block (like the Freedom Climb that was done to raise money and get publicity for a group of voluntary organisations in Bangalore on India's 50th Independence day).

♦ Something **directly related to the cause**, such as a sponsored litter pick for an environmental campaign (with sponsorship per kg of litter collected).

The event has to be appropriate to the age group and interests of participants. If students or teenagers are involved, a dance marathon (non-stop dancing through the night) would be appealing, especially if a well-known DJ agreed to host it. A health charity might organise a sponsored 'stop-smoking' initiative, where participants are sponsored for each day they continued not to smoke (say, up to a limit of 30 days, as the event has to have an end).

A Walkathon in Bangalore

In Bangalore in 1999, the Confederation of Indian Industry led a fundraising initiative in support of Karunashraya Hospice. Employees of CII and of some of CII's member companies participated in a **Walkathon** and raised over Rs 2.1 million for the hospice that serves terminally-ill cancer and AIDS patients.

The success of these events depends on:

♦ **Getting participants**; the more the better.

♦ Getting participants to **commit** to raising a certain level of sponsorship, and then providing them with publicity materials and encouragement to help them achieve their targets. They then have to sign up their family, friends and colleagues. If the event is really attractive, set more ambitious targets. Older people are better than students and schoolchildren at raising money. A stockbroker or management consultant can ask contacts and clients to sponsor him or her very generously, and such a request can be hard to refuse.

♦ You could even offer a **prize** for the person raising the most sponsorship as an incentive.

♦ For events that have a large element of fun in them, you might ask the **participant to contribute** something. For example, a sponsored parachute jump (run in association with a local flying club) might require the participant to contribute the cost of making the jump unless a certain target level of sponsorship was reached. The usual ratio for this sort of event is that the participant should raise at least four times the cost in order not to have to pay to participate.

◆ Ensuring that participants **collect the money** that has been pledged. This has to be done after the event, and really needs to be done as quickly as possible (within one month at the most). As organiser of the event, you must keep in touch with all the participants, and put pressure on them to collect the money.

Participants should be provided with **sponsorship forms**, so that people sponsoring them can commit themselves. These should give the following details:

◆ **Name** of sponsor.

◆ **Amount** of sponsorship. This can either be a fixed amount for participating, or the cost per unit completed (kilometre, lap of a running track, etc.).

◆ **Signature** of the sponsor.

TO DO   Organising an event

Think about some possible events that you might organise to raise support for your organisation.

1. Think of all the **different sorts of events** you could organise.

2. Decide which of your ideas you would like to pursue. Think about:

   • its **relevance** to your organisation as a fundraising event;

   • its **potential** for raising money, and the degree of risk involved (and whether there is a possibility that the event can be run successfully); and

   • whether you have the **skills and capacity** to organise the event successfully.

3. Start to **plan the event**. Think about all the steps you will need to take to turn the idea into action. Think about:

   • the **approvals** and the **resources** you will need, and what work you will need to do to get these;

   • a **draft budget** for the event: an outline sketch at this stage to give you an idea of the income and expenditure involved; and

   • the main **areas of difficulty** that need to be overcome, and how you will deal with these.

4. Design a **simple poster** for the event, asking people to participate or purchase a ticket.

◆ **Contact details** (which may already be known to the participant).

Every fundraiser needs to think about how to raise additional money from a fundraising activity. With a sponsored event, this is relatively straightforward:

◆ T-shirts can be printed and sold to participants and their supporters who come along to watch.

◆ The event and the T-shirts can be sponsored by a local business. An event often generates good publicity.

◆ Naturally everyone should be written to and thanked, and this provides you with the opportunity to ask them for additional support. The names and addresses of participants and their sponsors can be added to your mailing list. You can ask participants to participate in another fun event to be organised next year. You can show sponsors what their money has been able to achieve, and ask them to become regular supporters. They may have had little or no interest in the cause at the outset (having sponsored probably because a friend asked), but if you capture their imagination by putting on a fun-filled and well-organised event and promote your work in a lively way, then they might be happy to support you further.

Corporate donors

Why companies give

The following are some of the reasons for company giving:

◆ To **create goodwill in the local community**; to be seen as good citizens in the local communities where they operate, and as a caring company by society at large.

◆ To **create goodwill amongst employees**, who will get a good image from the good works that the company supports.

◆ To **be associated with certain causes**. Mining and extraction companies often like to support environmental projects, pharmaceutical companies like to support health projects, banks like to support economic development projects, and so on. This may be to enhance their image, but it could give them another perspective about matters that interest them.

◆ Because **they are asked**—and it is expected of them. They do not want to be branded as insensitive.

◆ A **special interest**: the Chairperson or other senior directors are interested in the cause (and perhaps support it personally). There is also the Chairperson's husband or wife who can play an important part through his or her interests and influence.

◆ **Publicity** for their products and for their 'corporate image'. Marketing and public relations are two important reasons why companies give. If you can deliver good publicity in return for their support, then they are more likely to want to give.

◆ **Tax**. There are tax reliefs on giving. This will be an added benefit for the company, but seldom the determining factor.

◆ **Entertainment opportunities**. This is why companies like to sponsor entertaining and sporting events; they can invite their important customers and suppliers.

Remember the following:

◆ It is the **shareholders' funds that are being given away**. For privately owned companies or companies that are largely owned and controlled by a family, giving by the company is little different from personal giving. But for public companies, the company will always want to be able to justify the support by being able to give a good reason for it.

◆ The **business of business is business**. Giving for charity and development is only a sideline activity. Companies do not have the staff to seek out and assess opportunities. They respond to the people they know and the requests they receive.

◆ Companies are usually only interested in **local projects** in areas where they have a business presence. They can then be seen to be a 'good corporate citizen' in the communities where they are located.

◆ If a **member of staff** is involved in some way – as a volunteer, through a family connection, etc. – this can be a good reason for the company to want to give.

◆ There is likely to be more money in the **marketing budget** or the **human resources budget** than in the **charity budget**. So, if you are proposing something that can help them with their marketing or employee relations, then they might be interested.

◆ Companies have a good business sense; they like to **give efficiently**. This means they are looking for ways of giving at little cost to themselves. A gift in kind of company products is one way of doing this.

◆ Companies **appreciate thanks, recognition and good publicity** for their support. And you can provide this by acknowledging their support in newsletters and in your annual report, and by trying to get press or media coverage for the activity they have supported.

What can companies give?

There are a variety of ways in which companies can support you. They can:

◆ Give a **cash donation**.

◆ **Sponsor an event** or activity.

◆ **Sponsor promotional and educational materials**.

◆ Engage in a **joint promotion**, where the company contributes a donation to the voluntary organisation in return for each product sold in order to encourage sales.

◆ **Make company facilities available**, including meeting rooms, printing or design facilities, help with mailing, etc.

◆ Give support **in kind**, by donating company products or office equipment that is no longer required. Giving things rather than money is often easier for a company.

◆ **Lend a member of staff** to work with your organisation, where a member of the company's staff helps on an agreed basis whilst remaining employed (and paid) by the company. This could be to provide some technical help (perhaps a 100-hour assignment), or to spend a longer period of time working with you (this is called 'secondment').

◆ Provide **expertise and advice**.

◆ Be involved **as a Board Member**. The company can agree to contribute a senior member of staff to serve in this capacity.

◆ Encourage **employees to volunteer**.

◆ Organise a **fundraising campaign amongst employees**. One method that is used in some countries is 'payroll giving'.

◆ **Advertise** in brochures and publications produced by the voluntary organisation.

There are two points to bear in mind:

1. **There are very many ways in which a company can help you.** This is an important difference from other funding sources, as most other funders can only give you money. So think carefully about the best way in which the company might help you. It is often easier (and less costly to them) for them to support you in some other way than a cash donation.

2. **There is an important difference between donation and sponsorship.** With a donation, the company gets nothing back except some form of thanks and acknowledgement. With sponsorship, the company aims to get a return for the money it is spending (publicity, opportunities for entertaining clients, improving its image through an association with a good cause, etc.).

What projects do companies like to support?

Companies support all sorts of projects. But the following are activities that they might be particularly interested in supporting:

◆ **Important local projects** in the areas where they have a significant presence.

◆ **Prestigious arts and cultural events**.

◆ **Sporting events and competitions**, especially those that attract keen public interest.

◆ **Activities that relate to their product**. For example, an ice cream manufacturer might want to support children's charities.

◆ **Economic development projects**—because a flourishing economy will benefit business.

- ◆ **Environmental projects**—because the environment is important for all.

- ◆ **Educational projects**. All companies value education, and this is something they like to support.

- ◆ **Emergency appeals**—because they feel they ought to contribute (to famine relief, for the victims of war, after an earthquake or flood, etc.).

- ◆ Initiatives that have **the backing of very prominent people**, including leading politicians. This is a way of gaining favour or access.

It is also important to know what companies are **unlikely** to want to support. Surveys suggest that most companies will not give to:

- ◆ **Local appeals outside the areas** where they have a business presence.

- ◆ **Religious appeals**, although this does not preclude supporting social development and community projects run by religious bodies. Where the Chairperson is a committed member of a religion, the company may be happy to give to a religious cause.

- ◆ **Circular appeals**, which are printed and sent out to hundreds of companies. These usually end up unread in the bin. You have to work hard at getting a personal message through to the person who can make a decision.

- ◆ **Controversial causes,** which might bring the company bad repute. They prefer to play safe, and they are seldom interested in supporting active campaigning bodies.

The types of companies that give

The types of companies that might be interested in supporting you include:

- ◆ **Leading national companies**. These include the banks and auto dealers, as well as manufacturing companies, shops and the service sector. Most leading national companies will be giving something to charity.

- ◆ **International and multinational companies**. Companies operating across the world often have a worldwide giving policy (this is true for most large US and UK companies).

- ◆ **Larger local companies**. In any city or region there will be large companies that are important to the local economy. These companies will often feel a responsibility to do something to support voluntary action and community initiatives in their area.

- ◆ **Smaller local companies**. If you are mounting a general appeal, then you will want to approach smaller companies for their support.

> **Getting in touch**
>
> To be successful, you need to do four things:
>
> 1. **Identify likely companies**.
> 2. **Identify the right project** for them to support.
> 3. **Find the appropriate person to approach** (the higher up in the company the better).
> 4. **Demonstrate your credibility** as a successful organisation (a successful company will want to be associated with a successful project).

How to identify likely companies

There are different ways of finding out about companies. You can:

◆ Make use of **existing contacts**. Find out who in your organisation (and on your Board) knows who. If you have volunteers or Board Members who work for companies, then get them to ask.

◆ Use **local knowledge**. If you are looking for an advertising agency, for example, to do some work for you for free, then who have you heard of locally?

◆ Look in the **business press** to see who's doing well, who's relocating in your area, who's expanding their business, who's just been awarded a major contract.

◆ Get hold of **trade directories**, which list companies in particular industries and sectors. The 'Yellow Pages' business **telephone directories** can also be used to identify local suppliers.

◆ Make contact with local and national **business associations**. The major networks are **Federation of Indian Chambers of Commerce and Industry** (FICCI) and **Association of Chambers of Commerce** (ASSOCHAM). These networks encourage their member companies to be socially responsible. Make contact with the local Director, and ask for advice. There are also many other business networks and associations at the city level, such as Lions, Round Tables and Rotary Clubs. At the national level there are two initiatives that promote corporate partnerships with voluntary organisations: (a) **Partners in Change**, which links companies to development projects, and (b) The **India Business-Community Partnership**, an Indian group linked to the Prince of Wales Business Leaders Forum, which is a network of leading companies, that support to community development.

You should try to identify companies that might be interested in you and your work. There is little information available on what companies are actually supporting. So, you should use common sense. For example:

◆ If you are looking for support for a micro-credit scheme, then a bank or financial institution might be interested—because of the business link between what you are doing and what they do.

◆ If you are looking for support for a rural development programme, then some large business in the area may be prepared to make a contribution or even 'adopt a village'.

◆ If you are looking for used office equipment or supplies to be donated to you, then major companies in your area would be the starting point.

◆ If you want free financial advice, then the leading firms of accountants should be approached, again in the area of the proposed project.

Industry associations

Industry associations are increasingly taking an interest in the idea of **corporate social responsibility** and **good citizenship** at the head office level, but as yet there is very little understanding of the concept at regional- and state-office levels. The main associations in India are:

• **Confederation of Indian Industry** (CII) India Habitat Centre, 4th Floor, Zone IV, Lodi Road, New Delhi 110 003.

CII organises dialogues, workshops, site visits and trainings; it networks around these issues, and plans to create a databank of successful business interventions and of projects that member companies might 'invest' in. CII has recognised the importance of promoting corporate social responsibility by establishing a committee, chaired by a leading business person, with five task forces to spearhead it.

• **Federation of Indian Chambers of Commerce and Industry** (FICCI) Federation House, Tansen Marg, New Delhi 110 001.

FICCI has a similar programme to that of CII; particular concerns are family welfare and women's issues. It is said to work through its regional chambers, encouraging them to develop community involvement initiatives with member companies according to local priorities. FICCI has recently decided to establish a socio-economic development foundation to institutionalise these.

• **Association of Chambers of Commerce and Industry** (ASSOCHAM) Allahabad Building, Sansad Marg, New Delhi 110 001.

Like FICCI , ASSOCHAM is said to actively promote corporate community involvement through local chambers. Population management is one of its main concerns.

Who decides and whom to write to

Practice varies from company to company.

◆ For **larger companies**, the decision on what to support will usually be taken by the Chairperson or Managing Director personally, or through some form of donations committee, which meets regularly to consider applications. Some very large companies operate an independent foundation, where the foundation and its trustees will set policies and decide on the applications. If you are looking for sponsorship, the Marketing Director or Brand Manager will be responsible for their marketing budget; or the company's advertising agency might put forward a proposal on your behalf.

Examples of corporate giving

- **Free office space**

Centre for Advancement of Philanthropy, Mumbai has for many years benefited from office space provided by Forbes Marshall—in the heart of Mumbai. The Slum Wing of the Delhi Development Authority gives Child Relief and You (CRY) rent-free use of one floor of the Community Facility Complex at Kotla Mubarakpur in New Delhi.

- **Free space for workshops and meetings**

CRY receives free space and facilities at the premises of J.J. Nursing Association at Aksa, Mumbai. It is worth mentioning that CRY has a policy to seek donations 'of anything, which can be donated' and 'to provide opportunities for people with all sorts of skills and abilities to contribute'. Because of this, CRY gets a very wide range of corporate and other forms of support.

- **Free use of database for mailing**

During 1997–98, the magazines *Business India* and *Inside Outside* shared their database with CRY, and Hutchinson Fax mailed CRY appeals to 50,000 of its customers.

For those who say 'it's alright for CRY, they are big and well known—but how can we do it as we just don't have their profile and resources', remember that CRY was started in 1979 by a group of five young people who jointly contributed Rs 50 to start the organisation.

- **Free advertising agency support**

A number of agencies provide support to voluntary organisations:

For some years, Lintas assisted Lok Kalyan Samiti (LKS) in New Delhi with their direct mail appeals for people to sponsor eye operations. Now LKS does its creative direct mail work itself—successfully.

R.K. Swamy has for some years provided design and advertising support to the Hindu Mission Hospital in Chennai.

In Bangalore, Ogilvy & Mather recently designed a new logo for the Association of Persons with Disability—they also design their newsletter and appeals.

- **Free management consultancy**

A.T. Kearney, a world renowned business consultancy, helped Deepalaya (which primarily works with children in the slums of Delhi), in 1997–98 by providing management consultancy to help with Deepalaya's organisational structure and human resource development systems. This support was facilitated by Partners in Change, an agency promoting business support for development.

◆ Many **multinationals** will have a manager who is given the responsibility of dealing with and deciding on charitable appeals—although the local top management may also have some say in what is supported. Sometimes, decisions are made by an international donations committee based at their international headquarters.

◆ For **medium-sized and smaller companies**, it is usually the top person who decides—the Chairperson or Managing Director.

The important point to note is that you should try to contact the person who has the responsibility for receiving and dealing with appeals.

If you have a personal contact, then you can telephone and ask for an appointment to present your case. Otherwise, you may have to write, although you can follow up the letter with a phone call to enquire whether the letter has been received (and even ask if you could come in to talk about your project).

You don't want to write to the wrong person, let alone someone who left the company 10 years ago! So check the name and job title before writing, by telephoning the Chairperson's Secretary.

Make sure the letter is brief. One page is usually sufficient—they are busy people. The letter should say who you are, what you do and why your work is important, why you are looking for money, and why they might be interested in supporting you. You can attach a leaflet or annual report (if you have one that is nicely written and designed).

How much to ask for

Companies are unlikely to want to make a huge donation—especially to an organisation that they have not heard of before. So it's best to think small when you are starting out. If you are approaching companies in a city, then Rs 5,000–Rs 10,000 would be a reasonable amount; Rs 50,000 would be a large donation, you should be very lucky to get this. If you are approaching a company in a smaller town or a rural area, then Rs 2,000 to Rs 10,000 might be the likely range.

Later on, when you have used their money successfully and begun to build up an excellent relationship, you can think bigger.

Getting support in kind

It is often easier, as stated earlier, for a company to donate some product or service, than to give money. If the company has what you need, then it will always be cheaper to give in kind rather than cash. And it is harder to refuse your request.

Here are some things that a company can donate:

◆ **Used equipment,** such as a computer or a fascimile machine or office furniture. Many companies replace their equipment quite frequently, and often do not know what to do with the old equipment they no longer require. What is not good enough for them, might be just what you need.

◆ **Services**, such as the professional services the company offers—which applies particularly to advertising and public relations agencies, accountants, and lawyers.

◆ **The use of equipment**, such as photocopying if you have a large report to bring out, the postage franking machine for a mailing you are doing, or the use of e-mail service (if you are not connected). These can either cost very little or the cost will 'get lost' and not be noticed.

◆ **The company's products**. Here you can make a special effort to publicise the donation, which the company will always appreciate. You can ask for products that you require for your work. You can also ask for things to use in fundraising events as gifts and prizes (like airline tickets and holidays from travel companies).

◆ **Raw materials** that the company uses, and this can include offcuts, which would otherwise be thrown away. Child Relief and You (CRY) runs a 'Materials Bank', in which things are 'deposited' by companies, gifts for use at children's organisations.

◆ **The use of company facilities**, such as the boardroom for an important meeting, or a training session. A company can also be asked to have a member of your staff attend an in-house training course, if they are organising anything that might be relevant to your needs.

◆ **The use of company expertise**. A member of staff such as a designer or a software expert could provide their services free. If you need to draw up a personnel policy, then the human resources director might be asked to help you. This help would normally be given in a voluntary capacity out of office hours. But you can approach the company formally to ask if they will allow you to ask and to find out who to ask.

Getting a gift in kind can be a first step in developing a closer relationship with the company, where they will support you on a regular basis. So say thank you and keep in touch. Treat a company that has supported you in kind, just as you would any other donor.

How to approach a company (and individuals) for support in kind is explained on page 90.

Payroll giving and getting donations from staff

Payroll giving is a method of raising money, where an employee agrees to have a regular amount deducted each month from his or her salary for donation to a charity. It is a very good form of fundraising because it involves a relatively long-term commitment by the donor, with the monthly contributions building up to a sizeable annual sum, and it provides the organisation with a predictable income. Payroll giving is well established in America and Singapore.

Two main forms of payroll giving are being developed in India.

The first is illustrated by the HelpAge scheme in Chennai. HelpAge goes into companies and asks employees to make a voluntary monthly contribution, deducted from their salaries. Funds go directly from the company to HelpAge.

The second is being developed by Charities Aid Foundation (CAF). CAF uses the brand name of **Give As You Earn** (GAYE). It first identifies a group of organisations representing a range of social and development activity. CAF then approaches companies and employees with the suggestion that they make a voluntary commitment to a particular cause/organisation of the individual's choice from the group selected by CAF. Monthly deductions are sent to CAF, who amalgamate donations from different companies and then send the donations to the selected voluntary organisations (less 10% administration charge—unless the company is willing to pay this).

In the first approach, the organisation gets the full benefit of the donation, but has to bear the full costs of running the scheme. A possible disadvantage to the employee is that he or she does not have a choice of causes. The advantage of the CAF scheme is that organisations not able to organise their own scheme can benefit; and employees have a choice of causes and organisations to support. The CAF scheme is in operation in Bangalore and in Delhi.

There are a few examples in India of a third variation of the scheme. This is where employees of an organisation make a voluntary donation either to their own work or to support an internal initiative of the organisation. For example, the staff of Paripurnata in Calcutta (a caring programme for women who have been held in prison for mental illness), make a monthly donation to support their own work—despite the fact that their salaries are low. It shows the commitment of the group to their own work and helps boost their confidence in asking others to contribute. Another example is a scheme run by the staff of the Meenakshi Mission Hospital, Madurai. About 1,000 staff make a voluntary monthly donation of Rs 5 or Rs 10 per head to a fund, from which patients who cannot afford mid-day meals are provided mid-day meals. Staff also take turns to serve the food. The scheme certainly helps strengthen the caring nature of the hospital.

Getting sponsorship

You need to understand the difference between donation and sponsorship. Sponsorship brings a return to the company, which is usually good publicity, but might also be the opportunity to advertise the company's products or to entertain important customers and clients.

When you are thinking about sponsorship:

◆ Think about **the benefit to the company**, and what it might be worth to them. Sometimes you can provide them with things that they could not get access to by themselves; a reception at the Raj Bhawan attended by a leading film actress as the 'star guest', for example.

◆ Set out the benefits clearly in a short (two-page) **project proposal**. Be as specific as you can. Don't just say, 'good publicity'. But make a list of the mediapersons you expect to cover the event and the expected viewership.

Sponsorship of cricket for the visually impaired

A voluntary organisation in Delhi called Society for Communication and Research (SCORE), is promoting cricket for the visually impaired in India, 'so that the visually impaired can enjoy the thrill of cricket'. The ball has jingles inside so that it can be 'seen'. National and regional tournaments have been held in different parts of India, and an international tournament was held in Delhi in 1998 which included teams from Australia and UK. All these events were sponsored by Coca Cola. These events added another dimension to Coca Cola's sponsorship of international cricket in India, showing it to be a caring company.

◆ Approach **the right person**. If the sponsorship will enhance the company's image, then approach the Chairperson. If it will promote the company's products, then approach the Marketing Director. And so on. Send the project proposal together with a leaflet about the work of your organisation, and any information on previous sponsorship that you have been involved with. Follow this up with a telephone call about a week later. Try to arrange a meeting.

◆ Start **sooner rather than later**. You will find that many budgets are already used up if you do it too late.

A variation on the idea of sponsorship is what is called a 'joint promotion'. Here your organisation teams up with a company to help sell its products or services. World Wide Fund for Nature (WWF) for example, partners a credit card company, so that for every credit card issued, a donation is made to WWF. WWF would make the names of its supporters available to the company to promote the credit card, and the company would also benefit from being associated with a good cause. Deepalaya teamed up with the Nirula's restaurant chain in a unique one-month fundraising programme. Diners were asked to donate the tip they would have left to Deepalaya. Child Relief and You (CRY) has worked with an auto dealer so that for each car sold on one particular day, CRY would receive a donation.

Getting companies to advertise

Companies are often prepared to support you by placing an advertisement in a brochure or a publication—possibilities include your annual report and the programmes you produce for fundraising events. Known as 'goodwill advertising', it is paid for to create goodwill for the company rather than sell more of its products.

Companies like advertising because they can treat the expenditure as a business expense; they get publicity in return for their support, they are being asked to give a specific amount, usually a sum that they can afford. Here are some tips on getting companies to advertise in a brochure or a publication:

1. **Prepare a 'rate card'** that gives the different rates for a full page, half page, etc.; work out an affordable price, yet which would generate a surplus for your efforts.

2. **Outline the sort of audience that the publication will reach**, and give some idea of the sort of benefits that the company can expect by advertising in your publication (reaching a select audience of decision-takers, or being distributed widely amongst your supporters, for example). This includes both the number of people as well as the sort of people who will see the publication.

3. **Approach companies that you think might be interested**. These would include those that have advertised in your publications previously, your suppliers, local companies keen to associate with your organisation, and companies where there is some connection between their business and what you do.

CASE STUDY   A rate chart for brochure advertising

Brochure advertising an entertainment event organised by the Hyderabad Council of Human Welfare (HCHW) in 1998 was offered at the following rates:

Front cover, half page	Rs	25,000
Back cover, full page	Rs	20,000
Full page	Rs	10,000
Half page	Rs	5,000
Quarter page	Rs	2,500

HCHW raised a total of Rs 90,000 through this brochure. Note the following:

*   **Premium rates** are charged for 'special positions', such as the back and front covers, which might also be printed in more than one colour. Also the 'inside front cover' and the page facing the table of contents can be sold at premium rates.

*   The rates in this example for a full page, half page and quarter page are proportional to the size of the advertisement space offered. But more money can be raised by **increasing the rates for smaller spaces**. Take an example, in which the full page rate is again Rs 10,000; the half page rate could be Rs 5,500 or Rs 6,000; and the quarter page rate Rs 3,000 or Rs 3,500. This pricing structure can encourage advertisers to book larger spaces.

4. **Follow up your original communication by telephone**, and tell them which other companies have agreed to advertise. Once you have got one company to agree, then it becomes easier to get others to decide to do the same.

5. **Offer to design the advertisement for them**. This is particularly useful if you are planning to approach smaller companies. You might even charge them a fee.

6. **Always show them a copy of the proof**, and get them to sign it as 'approved'. In this way, if there is a mistake, you cannot be blamed.

7. **Send them a copy of the publication**, with a note telling them on which page their advertisement has been printed.

8. **Make sure you get paid... and** say thank you.

Get in touch with local business leaders

Local business leaders may be pleased to know about what you are doing, proud of your achievements and willing to assist. But first they have to know of your existence. You should be aiming not just to get the support of a company, but to persuade local business leaders to back you. You might have room for one or two on your Board. They can then help you mobilise resources from the business community, which will be much more effective than acting alone.

◆   Approach **local Chambers of Commerce**, trade associations and other business associations. Of particular importance are foreign business grouping (such as a UK or US Chambers of Commerce). Embassies or Consulates will advise on this.

◆   Offer to **talk at meetings**, such as the Rotary Club, which often invite people from outside the business world to talk on a topical subject. This gives you a chance to meet people, and follow up on any expressions of interest.

◆   Select very few **prominent business leaders** to approach, who you think might be particularly interested in your work. Then find the best way of approaching them. A personal contact helps here.

TO DO   Which companies to ask

Think about some of the companies that might be interested in supporting you. Note down some ideas for the companies you might approach. Next to each company you list, identify something that you might ask them for. See if you have an existing contact with the company.

*   **International and multinational companies.**
*   **Leading national companies.**
*   **Larger local companies** operating near your project.
*   **Smaller local companies.**

What would you do if...

What would you do if...

You want to approach the Chairperson of a major company, but you don't know him or her, or have any existing contact with that company?

Answer:

- Ask your senior staff and Board if they know a senior person in the company that you can ask advice from.
- Contact the most important people you know to see if they know the Chairperson.
- Or if you have the personality and courage to do this...telephone the Chairperson's secretary and ask for an appointment, for just a few minutes in a busy day to see you.

What would you do if...

You need some legal advice without having to pay for it?

Answer:

- Make a list of some of the law firms you know of which you would trust, and if you know anyone senior in those firms, just ring up and ask. Or...
- ask your colleagues at work if they know anyone. Or...
- telephone the secretary of the senior partner of the most prestigious law firm you know and ask if you can have a short meeting as you desperately need some advice. This often works. And then you can use the meeting to ask for the help you need.

What would you do if.....

You are organising an auction to raise money and you want such things as holidays donated?

Answer:

- Prepare a letter with an information sheet on the event and a brochure about the work of your organisation.
- Find someone with a really good telephone manner to help you as a volunteer.
- Go through business and telephone directories to identify a target group of companies to ask for a range of products.
- Telephone the Chairperson or Managing Director's office and request to meet to discuss what you have in mind.
- Offer to send some information, if they can't decide then and there; say you will telephone again in about a week, once they have had a chance to read the information.
- Telephone again, just as you said you would.

Trusts and foundations

What are foundations?

Trusts and foundations are grant-making bodies set up specifically to give money for charitable purposes. They are usually endowed with a corpus, and distribute the income earned on this each year in grants. In some countries, foundations are an extremely important source of money for voluntary organisations. In India, however, there are not that many foundations to approach. There are some though, and it is possible to get a significant grant from a foundation if you can identify one that might be interested in what you are doing. Here are some foundations active in India:

◆ Major **international foundations**, such as the Ford Foundation and the Aga Khan Foundation, which have Indian offices based in Delhi.

◆ **National foundations**. The National Foundation for India (in Delhi), the Rajiv Gandhi Foundation (in Delhi) and the India Foundation for the Arts (in Bangalore) all make grants within their areas of interest. The National Culture Fund supports renovation and conservation of monuments in partnership with business. Child Relief and You (CRY) and Concern India Foundation are fundraising organisations that make grants with the money they are able to raise. CRY supports programmes that address children in need. Concern supports projects that address poverty and disadvantage. Both CRY and Concern have offices in major Indian cities which coordinate fundraising and receive applications from voluntary organisations in their area.

◆ Foundations attached to **major business groups**. Examples are the Sir Ratan Tata Trust, which is one of several important foundations attached to the Tata group of companies; the Levi Strauss Foundation, which has a representative in Bangalore, the company's India base. These company trusts are usually an extension of the company's own giving programme.

◆ **Local foundations** established to distribute money locally. The Bombay Community Public Trust and the United Way of Vadodara are two examples. The Chief Minister of Andhra Pradesh launched a major fundraising

Sir Ratan Tata, India's most celebrated philanthropist

drive in 1998 to create a foundation for targeting business leaders in the state and non-resident Indians.

◆ **Private foundations** established by wealthy (and not so wealthy) people as a vehicle for their philanthropy. Many of these exist, but you can only usually find out about them through personal contact.

Where to find out about foundations

In Mumbai, foundations from Mumbai and Maharashtra have been well documented by the Centre for Advancement of Philanthropy (CAP) and Indian Centre for Philanthropy (ICP). Both publish useful newsletters on philanthropy. For further information contact

• ICP at Sector C, Pocket 8/8704, Vasant Kunj, New Delhi 110 070; and

• CAP at Mulla House (Jehangir Wadia Building) 4th Floor, 51 M.G. Road, Flora Fountain, Mumbai 400 001.

What foundations support

Local foundations support local projects which address the problems of the city or region where they are based.

National and international foundations usually support national programmes, and they also support projects that are innovative and of national significance. They usually confine their support to one-off grants or recurrent grants made for a period of up to three years.

Private foundations support those projects that are of interest to the family running the foundation.

Under income tax rules, foundations are usually exempt from tax on the basis that they apply their money to **charitable purposes**.

The larger foundations have brochures that set out their giving policy and application procedure, with examples of the sorts of projects they have been supporting. There is little or no public information available about smaller and private foundations.

Approaching trusts and foundations

Find out about foundations. Find out whether there are any foundations which might be interested in supporting your work.

◆ Is your work of national significance and your organisation well known, and does your proposal fall within the guidelines of a national or international foundation?

◆ Is there an important local foundation active in your area?

◆ Do you have any contact with private foundations?

Research. If the answer to any of these questions is 'yes', then the next step is to find out as much as you can about their giving policy, the size of their grants and their application procedure.

◆ Some foundations will produce an annual report of their work, which gives details of their programmes and what they have supported.

◆ Some will produce simple guidelines for applicants.

◆ Others will not produce any information; so you will have to ask around to find out what they support.

Deciding what to ask for. Usually a well-defined project that addresses the need in an imaginative way is what will work best.

How two foundations give

The **Rajiv Gandhi Foundation** made grants of Rs 26.35 million in 1998. Its main areas of support in order of grants made were:

• **Literacy**, supporting various non-formal education projects and a village library programme.

• **Women and children**, with a street children programme in Indore and a vermiculture programme in West Bengal.

• **Project Interact** to assist lower income children who have lost one or both parents as a result of terrorist violence.

• **Disabled persons**, with support going to computer-aided teaching and rehabilitation, to run 'Lifeline' camps and for a motorised three-wheeler scheme.

• **Health**, with support going to AIDS/HIV initiatives, for cancer care at home, to a 'Health for All' social marketing initiative, and to healthcare for rickshaw pullers.

The foundation defines its programmes more by what it wishes to do than by responding to written applications.

The **Ford Foundation** is much larger. Since 1952 it has distributed $300 million in India through 2,400 grants. Its programme areas are:

• **Asset building and community development**, which covers land and natural resources management, livelihoods for poor people and women's sexual and reproductive health.

• **Peace and social justice**, which covers women's rights, police reform, Panchayati Raj support, regional reform and the promotion of philanthropy.

• **Education, media, arts and culture**, which covers folklore studies, new communications media and campus diversity.

An explanatory booklet with guidelines for applicants is available on request.

Applying. This might be a two- or three-page letter setting out your ideas and the sort of support you are looking for. This might be all that is required; or it could be a prelude to a meeting to discuss your ideas before submitting a formal proposal in the form they require. Some foundations have an application form, obtainable from them on request, which you will need to use. Procedures vary from foundation to foundation. If you are not sure what to do, then ask.

Raising money through overseas contacts and from tourism

In this section we look at some opportunities for raising money through some form of overseas linkage. The reasons why this can be an important source of funds are:

◆ People living and working overseas may have **higher disposable incomes**, and the difference is enhanced by the low foreign exchange value of the Indian rupee. So even small sums from the donor can be important for your work.

◆ The opportunity is there. **Tourism** can be used to develop fundraising, and the **non-resident Indians** (referred to as NRIs) living overseas have increasing wealth, which can be directed towards social and development projects.

Raising money from the overseas non-resident community

With increasing globalisation of business and as people migrate for economic or political reasons or seek educational opportunities away from India, there are more and more non-resident Indians (NRI) living abroad. Whether it is the Indian expatriate community in the Gulf or the NRIs in Europe and the United States, they all retain strong family links with their home country and culture. Even those Indians, mostly Gujaratis, who fled from East Africa in the 1960s have a strong emotional link with India.

This community represents an obvious fundraising source for charitable development and relief work being done in India (and in particular in the region or village where they grew up).

But how do you reach them, and what do you ask them to do?

There are a number of possible approaches. One is to **market your cause** to the non-resident community at large. This can be done through publicity in overseas Indian newspapers, by using networks in the country where they are now living, such as a Confederation of Indian Organisations, or through personal visits to develop your own contacts.

You can also use direct marketing. For example, HelpAge India used direct-mail fundraising (sending letters to address lists) to mobilise NRI support in the Gulf States, and Child Relief and You has arranged with banks to include an appeal with bank statements being sent to NRIs who hold rupee accounts with the bank.

Another approach is to **find an individual** who is interested in your work and wants to help by organising fundraising for you in their country. You might actively look for somebody, or you could just wait until someone appears. Here are some ideas to consider:

◆ **Contact the Indian Embassy** in the foreign country for details of business and community groupings, wives' associations (expatriates' wives are often at a loose end and want something interesting to do while their husbands are at work).

◆ **Use personal and family contacts.** It is surprising who you can get access to if you think about it or ask your friends. Most people when approached to do something useful are keen to do it! Many families now have members living abroad. Ask your senior staff and Board about their family members or friends who might be interested to support your work.

◆ **Go through your files** and **visitors' book** to see if there are any addresses of people you can contact. You can write to these people directly. But if there are quite a number of addresses, and you feel that they might be interested in doing something for you, then it might be worth making a trip to visit them.

◆ **Get coverage in the press**. There will often be newsletters or newspapers for the Indian community abroad that keep people in touch (with one another and with what's going on in India). Try to get your work covered in these. You could also write a letter to the editor, to be published on the letters-to-the-editor page, asking if anyone is interested in helping you with your fundraising.

◆ **Visit the country**—not to raise money in the first instance, but to make contacts, talk to groups and to see if you can find people prepared to help you.

If you do make a visit, take along plenty of explanatory brochures, and possibly a short video (perhaps lasting 10 or 15 minutes) showing your work. Give a contact point so that people can get in touch with you if they are interested. Follow up on every lead. Be persistent. You are there for only a limited time, the visit might have cost quite a lot, so you really do need a positive outcome.

You will want to identify people prepared to help you. Then ask them for support. Or you can ask them to set up a fundraising support group.

Setting up an overseas support group

If you can find people interested in helping you, you can ask them if they would be prepared to set up an overseas support group to raise money for you. They might raise money for you from among their own friends and contacts, and remit this to you.

Or they could consider setting up a society or trust in their country with charitable status as a vehicle for raising money and getting grants. A formal structure is advisable if they hope to raise large amounts of money and continue fundraising for you over a period of years.

The fundraising group can be started by a local person you have recruited, by an overseas volunteer returning home, or by a visitor to your project from abroad who has shown a particular interest in your work. They may want to recruit a few friends (say, between three and 10 people) to help them, and these people together will form the core fundraising group. Later on as the fundraising develops, the group can be expanded and even constituted as a charitable organisation with the purpose of raising money for your work.

Give the group **a project** (or several projects) to raise money for, and **a target** for the amount they will raise. You (and they) will be surprised by how much money can be generated in this way.

One simple thing they can be asked to do is to organise cultural evenings or dinner parties or entertainment events. Many non-residents are homesick and would welcome New Year's Eve parties or Diwali evenings when they could get together; and these can be organised as fundraising events for your work.

Another possibility is to ask them to apply to trusts, foundations and other sources of money in their own country which are available for overseas development work.

You will need to keep in regular contact with the group, so that they can see how your work is developing. They will need literature, which you could provide or which they could have printed. A short video will also be extremely useful in helping them gather support. You may find later that a number of the 'supporters' they recruit come to visit you or even volunteer to work with you.

Some examples of overseas support groups

Louise Nicholson was approached to set up a support group for a children's charity in Calcutta. Louise Nicholson is a well-known travel writer, author of a leading guidebook to India and brings groups of travellers to India. Louise organises 'charity dinners' to raise money for the project, when guests pay for the cost of the dinner (in a restaurant) and are then asked to make a donation.

The Karuna Trust is a charity set up in the UK, which supports an orphanage in Pune. They raise money by going from house to house, knocking on doors to find if people are interested, then recruiting supporters who are prepared to give regularly over a period of years.

Michael Norton met the Director of CHILDLINE, a telephone helpline in Mumbai for street children in need, and was impressed with their work and their wish to extend the service into other cities. He organised an application to the National Lottery Charities Board in the UK for a grant towards their expansion across India, and established a partnership with ChildLine, an organisation in the UK doing similar work, for joint research and international advocacy.

The potential of tourism and tourists for raising money

In many countries, tourism represents an extremely important contributor to the national economy. Some tourists are on tightly organised schedules and never stray from their group, while others are more adventurous and may well be tempted to share some interesting experience which you can devise for them.

There will also be people who are already interested in the sort of work you are doing and make a point of visiting you—you have a special opportunity to enlist their support. Here are some ideas:

Visitors to your project

Visitors can be people passing through, who have heard about your work, or people coming on a tour organised by a donor agency for its committed supporters to see some of the projects they are helping. Or if you run a conference or training centre, there are the people attending events run at the centre. These people are clearly interested in what you are doing, which is a good starting point.

You have a chance to show them your work, and to ask them to support you. Make sure you have a visitors' book (where they can write their name, address and e-mail), give them publicity material about your work, ask them if they are interested in doing something for you when they return home—you can even ask them to make a donation then and there.

Attracting tourists

You can try to attract tourists to visit you by arranging events and activities at your project (with transport laid on if required).

Some tourists would like to do something 'out of the ordinary' during their stay, which brings them closer to the life of the country they are visiting—visiting local craftsmen at work (and perhaps buying what they produce), seeing a rural development project, being shown round a museum with a talk from an expert. The opportunities are endless!

What you might try to do is to arrange to have a leaflet or even display a panel about your organisation and its work in local hotels. This could give details of the events and activities you are organising, as well as explain your work and encourage people to visit you.

You could even design special events such as a cycle tour of the city, or a visit to see parliament in action. Even where this bears little or no relation to your work, you will be organising something interesting that tourists would want to do, and this will give you the opportunity to explain your work and gain their interest.

If these events are organised regularly, then you can think about writing to the main guide books used by foreign tourists (such as *Lonely Planet* or *Rough Guide Footprints*). Visit a bookstore to see what is available and to get the address of the publisher—but it may take up to two years to get listed.

ACCORD asks its visitors for support

Action for Community Organisation, Rehabilitation and Development (ACCORD) is a tribal development project in South India. It runs a hospital and a community health service as part of its work. This is supported in part by an insurance scheme where families pay a small monthly contribution. It aims to be as self-sufficient as it can. But there is always a need for money to cover running costs, to purchase equipment or for new developments. ACCORD receives a steady stream of overseas visitors. They have developed a sponsorship scheme, whereby a visitor can sponsor the hospital and health work for one day at a cost of US$50. They will then write to you and tell you what happened on that day—what they were able to achieve with your money. How many babies were born, what operations took place, what lives saved, etc.

Returned volunteers

Some organisations have foreign (and Indian) volunteers working with them for a summer, for a year, or for a longer period. When these volunteers return home, they can be extremely helpful to you in your fundraising. They are already enthusiastic about your work, so your job is to build on that enthusiasm. You can do a number of things:

◆ Suggest that they form a **local support group** *(see above)*.

◆ If they are going back to paid employment, they might like to make **a regular and substantial financial contribution** to your work—perhaps a small percentage of what they earn. They may not have thought of that. So discuss the possibility with them before they leave.

◆ They may be able to help you **access sources of money** in their country, particularly from foundations. If **you** were to write to the foundation, you would almost certainly get rejected—not because your project is no good, but because they have no way of assessing your application from such a distance. If **they** write, then that provides a point of reference. The fact that they have worked for you, gives them an enthusiasm and enhances the chances of the application succeeding.

◆ They may be able to **link you with other organisations**—for example, a school in their country which can adopt your project and fundraise for it; or a voluntary organisation which has just the expertise you need.

Raising money from overseas contacts

Seva Mandir works in 535 villages in Udaipur district in Rajasthan. It promotes health, literacy, natural-resource management, afforestation and women's development. In a period of 18 months up to September 1998, it had 10 foreign volunteers staying for periods ranging from two weeks to six months, and eight visitors from Europe and North America as well as a group of two teachers and 10 students from the UK.

This exposure to overseas volunteers and visitors is reflected by a sum of Rs 984,000 received in donations from 10 foreigners during the same period. This included Rs 99,050 ($2,000) donated by an American couple who had made a study visit to look at Seva Mandir's educational and development efforts, and a total of Rs 789,318 collected by the Friends of Seva Mandir, a support group in the UK.

Government sources

Alongside the foreign donors who have been providing much of the funding for development work, there will also be government sources at national and state level (and local government sources at district or panchayat level) that are available for your work. The process of getting support is very similar to getting support from an international donor agency *(see the next section)*.

◆ Research to find out **what's available**, the policies, procedures and timetable for distributing the money of any likely grants scheme. Remember that funds may be available at all levels of government.

◆ Identify **the person** who will be responsible for receiving applications and making a decision on your proposal. Personal contact should be used if possible, as this enables you to make a much more powerful case as well as build a rapport with them. You need people who can lobby government effectively and who are able to develop good relationships with the civil servants who will be processing your proposal as well as with the politicians who are responsible for the particular area of work. But don't overdo things. Be professional in your relationships, and set high standards of integrity in your dealings.

◆ Understand their **motivation for giving**, and how you might be able to help them deliver a programme or meet a need that they are responsible for. This will help you build a good case for support.

Why government funds voluntary organisations?

There are a number of reasons why government might fund a voluntary organisation:

◆ There is a **budget line** for this purpose. For example, the government funds Council for Advancement of People's Action and Rural Technology (CAPART) to make grants to voluntary organisations for rural development. Knowing what's available is extremely important. Getting this information early on is also important, as many budget lines are time constrained (they may be available only in the financial year ending 31 March, or within a Five-Year Plan).

◆ A voluntary organisation can deliver service **more effectively** than a government department. This is becoming recognised, but does not apply to all voluntary organisations—as some are inefficient or corrupt. You will need to demonstrate your effectiveness.

◆ There is a possibility of creating a **working partnership**. Many of the joint forestry management programmes use voluntary organisations for extension work and to run training programmes for forest communities in partnership with the Forest Department.

◆ A voluntary organisation can bring **additional funds** into the programme through its own fundraising efforts.

◆ A voluntary organisation may be able to offer an **innovative approach** to dealing with the problem.

◆ The **government wants to do something**, and uses the voluntary organisation as the implementing agency because of its expertise and experience, and because of its ability to respond quickly.

Where to find out about government support

The Government of India has a large number of schemes to support social and development needs. Each scheme has its own focus and criteria for application. One important scheme is Jawahar Rozgar Yojana (JRY), which aims at (a) improving and expanding employment opportunities for the rural landless, (b) creating durable assets for the poor, and (c) improving the quality of life in rural areas especially through social forestry, water harvesting and land development.

The expansion of CHILDLINE

CHILDLINE is an emergency telephone helpline for street children in need or facing a crisis. It was developed in Mumbai, and with funds from the UK was set to expand to six metro areas. At this stage, the Government of India became interested, through the Ministry of Social Justice and Empowerment. They saw CHILDLINE as an opportunity to provide a basic service for vulnerable children across India, and enlisted the support of UNICEF who had already funded some of the training programmes run by CHILDLINE for health workers and the police. The result has been an agreement between CHILDLINE and the Government of India—the government and UNICEF will fund a four-year development programme to extend CHILDLINE services to 45 cities.

A comprehensive source of information on government schemes is the publication, *Development Programmes and NGOs*, which is a guide to central government programmes for NGOs in India. This is available from Bangalore Consultancy Office, No. 680 15th Main, 38th Cross, 4th T Block, Jayanagar, Bangalore 560 041.

Donor agencies

One recent trend in donor aid is the decentralisation of decision-making to regional and local offices in the respective countries. More and more funding from international donor agencies is (a) being given to non-governmental organisations rather than on a government-to-government basis and (b) being accessed locally in India by the Indian branch of a development agency (such as Oxfam or Christian Aid) in partnership with a local voluntary organisation or by local voluntary organisations directly.

This means that it is no longer sufficient for a voluntary organisation simply to develop a project and leave it to another agency to access the funding from Northern donors. Your organisation has to understand how donor agency support works and the principles of fundraising from this source. You will also need to play an active part (with your partner development agency or on your own) in the fundraising process.

Why do donor agencies give?

One key difference between a donor agency and many other types of givers is that they have already allocated a sum of money to give away, and they usually have to give this away before the end of their own budget year.

Many donor agencies also have a 'thrust' to their giving programme: Their own reasons for giving and a vision for what they want to achieve; their own policies and priorities for what they want to support; their own style of partnership with the organisations they are funding. Some have a particular ethical or religious basis to their work; others may want to work through their own networks and contacts; and some large agencies such as World Vision and PLAN International focus on child sponsorship, where they link donors with children from the communities they operate, as this is used as the way of raising money for their development work.

Donor agencies are looking for:

◆ **Projects and initiatives that fit within their programmes**, policies, priorities and guidelines. These are usually published. They may also have a 'focus area' (such as one or a group of states), to which they prefer to make grants.

◆ Projects with the sort of **budgets** they are happy to give to. Some agencies do not have sufficient funds to commit $100,000 a year for five years. For others, this amount would be a small grant.

◆ Specific **measurable outcomes and impact**. You should be able to demonstrate how much you are going to achieve with their money.

◆ Organisations with a **track record of success and good management**. Conversely, they are looking to avoid organisations that have wasted money or are believed to be corrupt.

◆ **Innovation**, where there is a really good idea to solve a problem that they are interested in. It is good to be 'at the cutting edge'.

◆ Projects that are **fashionable**. Every generation throws up ideas, which become common currency amongst development agencies. At the moment some such ideas are community empowerment, watershed management, participatory appraisal, gender issues, income generation, micro-credit, and capacity building. Advocacy and rights work is growing in importance.

◆ A degree of **professionalism**. This means talking the right language (i.e., not using jargon that individuals and companies would not understand), and using techniques (such as log frame analysis), which they are used to.

◆ **Dissemination of any learning**. This can spread the fact that they have backed a 'winner', as well as ensuring that others will benefit from your experience.

◆ An **evaluation** of the results of the work and its long-term impact, which should be built into the budget for the project.

◆ A **working partnership**. This usually means that they wish to exercise a greater degree of control over how you run the programme, than either an individual or a corporate donor would.

◆ **Transparency and accountability**. This covers a whole range of matters from accounting and clear presentation of financial information, regular reporting back, an evident lack of corruption, equal opportunities, reasonable (not too high) salaries, etc. They will want to see an annual report that shows the organisation in good shape. Many are giving away public funds, and need assurance that their money is not misused.

◆ A **properly constituted organisation** with permissions to receive foreign funds.

Getting in touch

To be successful, you need to do the following things:

1. **Identify likely donors**, and find out as much as possible about their programmes, timetables, and the procedures for writing an application. You need to be sure that what you are planning fits their interests, their policies and their geographical focus. The more initial research you do, the better.

2. **Develop the right project for them** to support—which can require a lot of creative thought.

3. **Find the appropriate person to approach**. Many donor agencies have decentralised their giving into the countries where they are spending the money, where they have programme directors or grants officers for you to liaise with. If they are giving from their own country, they may require that you work with a partner organisation based in their own country.

4. **Demonstrate your credibility** as a successful and lively organisation with an excellent track record of success.

5. If you can, **discuss your proposals** with them first, so that you know what they are looking for, you can then highlight these factors when you submit your application. You can also discuss the size of the project and your budget. It is always better to make personal contact with a potential donor, rather than just writing in. But if you are not able to arrange a meeting, send an outline proposal. You can always telephone later on to see if this has been received and also ask whether a meeting would be helpful.

6. **Fill in the application form** (if they have an application form), answering every question in a sensible way. Or write a proposal setting out your case.

Most international donor agencies and embassies, which handle grants to voluntary organisations in India (most embassies have a First Secretary with this role), are based in Delhi. This puts Delhi-based organisations at an advantage, as they may already be known to the people they are approaching. If your organisation is from outside Delhi, you are at a distinct disadvantage. One way of doing something about this is to make a trip to Delhi to try and arrange meetings with people you have identified as potential donors.

Doing the research

To find out about donor agencies that might be interested in receiving an application from you, you could:

◆ Consult a **funding directory**. A number have now been produced in India. However, many directories are out of date or inaccurate even at the time they are

---

Getting known in the capital city

The Centre for Development Communication (CDC) makes audio-visual programmes on development issues for training and advocacy work. It also runs communication skills training courses. It is a national organisation based in Hyderabad. It has arranged with the Canadian High Commission in Delhi to organise meetings with donors, to explain its work to them and become better known to potential donors.

published, so you may need to check the information. Most are not comprehensive, and only include information from sources that have replied to their questionnaire. So your own knowledge can add to the information gleaned from directories.

◆ Identify **organisations similar** to your own, and then find out who they have been receiving funding from. These might lead you to one or two sources you had not previously considered.

◆ Ask your **existing funders**. There may be an informal network of donor agencies, and they might know, which other funder might be potentially interested in supporting you, and even 'put in a good word for you'.

◆ If you belong to a **religious network**, ask around the network.

◆ If you are interested in receiving money from a **particular country**, because you have a link with that country, ask the embassy to suggest suitable agencies. Or ask a volunteer from that country to do some research for you when they return.

From all this research, you will need to get the name of the donor agency, its address and telephone number, the name of the person to write to with their job title, and a brief description (if you can get it) of their funding policies.

At this stage you will have found out as much as you can about the donors to see whether it is worth your while to approach them. You particularly need to know about the focus of their grants programme and the geographical area where they make grants. Write a short letter of no more than a page, outlining who you are and what your organisation does, what you are planning and the amount of financial support you are looking for. It is better to write, as donor agency staff are under constant pressure of people phoning or faxing. This not only creates annoyance, but many have no capacity to deal with these enquiries. On the other hand, if a letter gets put into the system, it will be dealt with in due course. If you don't get a reply within a month, then try telephoning. In your letter ask for a copy of any statement of policy that they have for supporting development work, details of application procedures and timetables, and a copy of their latest annual report.

You will then be able to draw up a short list of donor agencies, where you consider that there is a real chance of getting support. Concentrate your efforts on these.

Getting support in kind

As has been explained in the section on getting support from companies, it is often easier for a company to give you support in kind than it is for them to make a cash donation. It is also a good proposition to ask individuals to give you things rather than money.

Here are some practical tips on how to set about getting support in kind.

1. **Make a list of everything you need**—this is called a 'wish list'. This can include services as well as products (such as the design for the leaflet you plan to produce).

2. Go through the list and **try to identify companies** and **individuals** who might have what you require. For things like used office equipment, approach larger companies. For gifts of product or services, approach those companies that have what you need. Personal knowledge of who might have what, is a first step. But you can also do research, by using business directories or going through business networks.

3. **Make contact**. Writing a letter does not work well, as letters tend to get thrown away. It is best if you can make personal or telephone contact with the person who is able to make an immediate decision on your request. Usually, the higher up in the company, the better. But if there is something you particularly need, go to the person who can make the decision to give you what you need. State your request, saying that it is for a good cause indicating how much you need it and how well it will be used.

4. Even if a company refuses to donate what you are asking for, they might be able to give you a **substantial discount** (perhaps half price). This is worth getting. And can be a fallback position in your discussions.

5. **Be positive and enthusiastic**. It can be very difficult for anyone to refuse if they know what you want and how important it is for you. It will always cost them far less to donate the item than it would cost you to purchase it. This is a point you can make when you are asking.

6. **Say thank you**. Report back subsequently on the difference the donation has made. Put them on your mailing list. Send them a copy of your annual report each year. Try then to recruit them as cash donors.

An example of a wish list

The following is a short wish list drawn up by a training and support agency for voluntary orgnisations:

*   A website specialist to do a one-week consultancy.
*   Up-to-date (and legitimate!) software.
*   A good quality laser printer.
*   Two volunteers to do one day a week each; office administration and bookkeeping.
*   Strategic planning assistance; a person who could give half a day to 'follow up work'.
*   A meeting room (for up to 20 people), in or near the heart of the city, to use between 5.00 p.m. and 7.30 p.m. once in a week, for fundraising advice sessions.

Having defined your 'wishes', do something to realise them. Get on the telephone now!

Using volunteers

Volunteers can play a really important role in your organisation, bringing person-power to your work at far lower costs than recruiting a member of staff. There is a cost involved in using volunteers though, as volunteers need supervision (this has to be professional), and you will probably want to pay their expenses.

At the head office, volunteers can be used for general help around the office, for their expertise or to provide a particular service (for example, a lawyer may give free legal help to a rape crisis project), to assist with fundraising (either on a continuing basis or to help out at a particular event), or even by becoming a board member of your organisation.

Some examples of how volunteers can be used

1.   Mobilising professional skills

Society for Service to Voluntary Agencies (SOSVA) in Pune, is a support centre for voluntary organisations, and runs a volunteer recruitment service, mobilising people to support social causes and then placing them with organisations that can use their skills. In the 18 months till end-1998, 350 volunteers were mobilised. One is a gentleman who cycles 12 km each way every Saturday to shave the inmates of an old-age people's home. He has been doing this for 12 months so far.

Another example is that of an advertising agency executive in Mumbai who provides professional guidance to voluntary organisations with their annual reports.

2.   An action campaign to save lives

'We are a group of nobodies from Maharashtra. A group of common people. All of us work hard for a living; some of us are managers and senior officials, some still students, some housewives, some employees of major companies, some private practitioners. We used to read about the deaths of Korku children in Melghat every year. We also read about the efforts that the government was taking to prevent these deaths. We wondered, in spite of these efforts, 'why the number of deaths each year kept increasing?'

This was the start of an action campaign to save children's lives. The group calling itself Melghat Mitra (friends of Melghat), went to Melghat in May 1998 determined to prevent the death of every single child in seven villages caused by malnourishment during the critical monsoon period. Many daily newspapers published their appeal, and a popular Marathi daily carried a feature. Over 3,000 people responded, offering donations, skills and time. Rs 350,000 was raised through their generosity. 200 volunteers agreed to give 10 days of their time to the project (one day for orientation, two for travel, and seven spent in the villages) over a period of 92 days. Mission accomplished!

Now Melghat Mitra is tackling the long-term development needs of the villages they got involved with. Three volunteers have now been there for six months. Where will it all lead?

Many organisations also mobilise volunteers at grassroots levels for programmes they are running. Some may be doing work for free; others may be paid a small honorarium. Either way, you are adding value to the money you are spending on the programme. Your volunteers are a resource that you have been able to mobilise. Although this is not the same as getting cash support, it is of immense value.

It is worth thinking about the value of your volunteers. You can calculate this roughly by adding up the number of volunteer hours you are mobilising and marking an average salary against it (for professional help, you could even put the rate for the job that you would otherwise have had to pay). This is the value of the resource you have mobilised, and you should be telling your funders about it—even when you are fully funded by large grants. It makes their grants more effective (as you would be able to deliver the programme at a lower cost), it saves money (so you need to do less fundraising), and it creates an activity in which there is more commitment from the people involved.

Income generation

Income generation is another important area of resource mobilisation—although the details of running an income-generation activity successfully is really beyond the scope of this book. You can develop income from the following sources:

◆ By **levying a charge for the service** you are providing. People can make a contribution for health or education, or a micro-credit programme can include a management charge as an overhead. Some organisations believe that even the very poor can pay something, and that giving them a financial stake in the service creates a better working relationship for both parties. It is no longer seen as 'charity', and there are expectations on you to deliver a suitable level of quality as they are partly paying for it.

◆ By **selling products from projects**, although you will want to see as much of the income going back to the producers. Some development projects can be made largely self-financing from the income they generate from the sale of craft items and other produce.

◆ Through **selling expertise**—this includes publications, training and consultancy. Some organisations also have training centres, which they hire out to generate an income.

◆ Through **sideline trading** activity that you develop with the specific idea of generating an income for your work. This can be a difficult area as it is often easier to lose money than it is to make some. In India, many voluntary organisations are trying to use the sale of greetings cards to generate income, and most end up losing money.

A WWF greetings card

We will discuss two kinds of income-generation activities, which many voluntary organisations get involved with or may be considering in the context of fundraising:

1. greetings cards; and

2. selling expertise.

Sale of greetings cards

A number of voluntary organisations produce and sell greetings cards very successfully: Child Relief and You (CRY), UNICEF and Concern India Foundation all sell cards on a national level, and this has become a primary source of their income. Others, like Lok Kalyan Samiti (LKS) produce greetings cards to sell to an existing mailing list of active supporters. In both these circumstances, it is possible to earn good money from the sale of greetings cards.

But many smaller voluntary organisations, seeing the success of these operations, assume that producing greetings cards is an easy way to earn money, so they set about doing this themselves. They make mistakes at every point:

◆ They have **no list of supporters to sell to**, and **no sales network** (such as shops prepared to display and sell cards, or volunteers prepared to sell house-to-house).

◆ They have **no eye for design**, and select illustrations that people will not buy.

◆ They get the cards printed to a **poor standard** and at a **high cost**, because they have no experience.

◆ They **do not mark up the price sufficiently**, meaning that there will be insufficient margins over the costs.

◆ They produce too few cards, of too many designs. A **small print run** means that the unit cost of each card is too high; and they can't even sell the small quantities that they produce, so that they are **left with unsold stock**.

The end result is that the organisation ends up losing rather than making money. Selling greetings cards is not usually a good idea unless you have a method of selling, can produce good quality cards with nice designs, and are able to get the printing done cheaply so there is sufficient margin to generate adequate profit.

CASE STUDY Greetings cards

The SOSVA experience

Society for Service to Voluntary Agencies (SOSVA) provides assistance and training in NGO management, fundraising and volunteering. Seeing the success of CRY and UNICEF in greetings cards, in 1994 SOSVA decided to try to raise money this way. It produced 3,000 copies of a catalogue featuring around 30 cards, and printed 4,000 copies of each card. The approximate costs per card were as follows:

Design and printing	Rs 3.50
Envelopes	Re 0.20
Catalogue and mailing	Rs 1.23
Administration	Re 1.00
Total	**Rs 5.93**

Cards were sold by distributing catalogues and through bulk orders from the Karnataka and Delhi chapters of SOSVA and from NGOs assisted by SOSVA. The retail price was Rs 7, and cards were sold in bulk for resale at Rs 4.50—below the cost price.

It is hard to make money from greetings cards, unless the operations are carefully controlled.

- SOSVA finds that some designs sell really well and reprints are needed, but others sell not so well (although the unsold stock can be held over until the following year).

- Margins are slender, meaning that costs need to be rigidly controlled. Also, for such a small operation, costs will be higher than when tens of thousands of each card are being printed. So you need to be sure that there is a sufficient market for your cards before opting for this form of fundraising.

- This operation requires administration. Two office assistants and one accounts clerk are taken on for 2–3 months. All this needs to be budgeted for.

Greetings cards and stationery items produced by SRUTI

Society for Rural Urban and Tribal Initiatives (SRUTI) supports nearly 100 fellows engaged in community development, by offering them technical and financial assistance. One of its fundraising activities is the production and sale of greetings cards and stationery. These were initially handmade from cloth and paper scraps received via its newspaper/raddi collection scheme. But the operation has expanded and the card and cloth are now purchased.

The greetings cards sell at Rs 10 and Rs 6; postcards at Rs 5 each; envelopes and paper bags are also sold. A boy with the required skills is employed to make the products. 1997 saw sales worth Rs 82,000 against the production/administration cost of Rs 48,500 (a profit margin of 40%). The products are marketed through various *melas* and fairs and through select book and gift shops.

The design element here is important, as is a competitive market. Most people will purchase these items because they like them, rather than to support a cause.

Selling your expertise through training, consultancy and publications

Many voluntary organisations are doing important innovative work, and find that there is a demand from other organisations:

◆ to hear about their work and to learn from it;

◆ to advise on programme design and implementation;

◆ to train programme staff in working methods;

◆ to assist in the delivery of the programme by providing a service under contract (such as training extension workers).

Many voluntary organisations are also interested in documentation and dissemination—recording their working methods and spreading the message.

All of these activities can be undertaken to generate income, whether on a cost-recovery basis or to generate a surplus, which can then be used to fund other work of the organisation. This form of income generation has the advantage that it promotes the objectives of the organisation and at the same time raises money for it.

There are a number of issues that should be addressed:

◆ Does your organisation have the **legal power** to trade? This will normally be included as a power in the constitution. Sometimes organisations are not sure. Sometimes they are cautious, believing that there might be legal/tax implications if they were to sell their services. For example, Youth for Unity and Voluntary Action (YUVA), which works with vulnerable children in Mumbai, has a publishing programme, but instead of giving a price for its publications, it indicates a 'suggested contribution'. Note also that under Foreign Contributions Regulation Act (FCRA) rules, voluntary organisations in receipt of foreign funds are not allowed to publish and sell periodical publications (so their periodicals are usually designated 'for private circulation only').

◆ Is your organisation **happy with the idea** of 'trading'? Some organisations come from a strong anti-capitalist tradition, and instinctively dislike the idea of selling anything for gain. Others are so used to the idea that publications and training should be provided and obtained free, that they have never considered the idea of charging or paying.

There are, however, many advantages of selling expertise or a service:

◆ It forces you to do your **costing**. You have to know how much it costs you to provide the service, before you can decide how much to charge for it. This in turn helps you manage the activity better.

◆ It forces the purchaser to make a **positive decision** to make a purchase. This means that they will read the publication or attend the conference. Many free publications are discarded unread. Many people do not turn up at conferences where they have been booked for free.

◆ It forces the provider to provide what the participant or purchaser **wants or needs**.

◆ There is a link between **price charged and perceived value**. If it's expensive, many people believe it will be good. If it's free, they may feel it has no value.

◆ You can always have **differential pricing** to allow for the different purchasing power of different purchasers (for a publication, you might have different rates for overseas selling and for sale in India; or different rates for commercial, government and voluntary organisations).

◆ You can always make a positive decision to give **free places** or send **free copies**. But this then becomes part of your marketing or dissemination strategy.

How to do your costing

Many people do not know how to charge for services. Many undercharge, which means the more they provide, the more it costs them. This is negative income generation! We suggest some simple ways to help you calculate how much to charge.

Charging for consultancy

Many voluntary organisations have no idea how much to charge for undertaking consultancy. There is a simple formula that you can use to calculate a reasonable daily consultancy rate, which is based on the following calculations:

1. There are 260 weekdays per annum

2. From this, deduct 20 days for public holidays, which leaves 240 days available for work.

3. Half of this time is spent on some or all of the following: sick leave and time off including casual holidays, attending meetings and conferences and doing routine administration work. This leaves only half the working year available for 'productive work', which amounts to 120 days per year.

4. If your monthly salary is Rs 10,000, this is equivalent to Rs 120,000 per annum.

5. The cost of your time for each consultancy day is therefore Rs 1,000.

6. But you should at least double this to allow for normal benefits and organisational overheads.

7. So for every Rs 10,000 of your salary, your daily chargeable rate should be Rs 2,000. For example, if your salary is Rs 25,000, your daily chargeable rate should be Rs 5,000; if the salary is Rs 7,000, the rate should be Rs 1,400 a day.

This is how to calculate a realistic charge out rate. If you feel this is too expensive, you can always decide to reduce the rate, but you will be doing this with the knowledge that you are having to subsidise the cost of the consultancy out of your other income.

You might decide that it is too low a rate, and that you should actually be charging more. Check how much others are charging, in particular how much other voluntary organisations and non-profit providers are charging and also how much commercial providers charge. This can give you a reference for setting your own charges.

Charging for training

If you provide training, you need to think about how much to charge for it. The cost of training includes the venue, the cost of the trainers, the handouts and other materials. It also includes the cost of marketing the event, including producing a brochure; the cost of supervising the event, including the cost of attendance at the event; and the administration and overhead costs of the training provider.

We suggest that at 1999 prices, a reasonable daily charge for training senior staff might be around Rs 500–700 per person. This would not include the cost of overnight accommodation, breakfast and evening meals, which could be charged to the participant at extra cost. Travel to the venue would be the participant's responsibility. For lower-level training, the charges would need to be set lower. For very complicated events, such as those where a computer is needed by each participant or where expensive materials are consumed, the rate might need to be raised.

At this rate, you ought to be able to cover your costs. You should do a budget, basing the predicted income on the expected number of participants. Even if you charge, this does not preclude you from offering free or subsidised places, which you can do by having a limited number of bursaries or a reduced rate for certain types of organisation. But you will need to allow for these bursaries or reduced fee places in your budget.

CASE STUDY   How CDC charges for training

The Centre for Development Communication (CDC) Hyderabad, organises practical skills training workshops in communication for voluntary organisations. Print and audio-visual media is used extensively. Workshops normally last from two days to one week. CDC charges approximately Rs 700 per day, which is divided into a non-returnable registration fee payable on registration and a course fee payable before the course starts. The additional cost for boarding and accommodation is charged out at cost (approximately Rs 400 per day). The main consideration for CDC is the quality of training. People will come if the course provides something useful and if CDC maintains its reputation as a training provider of national standing. Price has not been a constraint. Most voluntary organisations now have training budgets, or can find the cost of training (a good part of which will be travel to and from the venue).

Pricing publications

A simple rule of thumb for pricing a publication is 'one third production; one third marketing; one third distribution'. The **research and writing** will normally be absorbed in the organisation's costs or be funded through a specific grant.

The **production** cost includes editorial work, illustrations or photographs, design and printing. This represents about one-third of the work that is needed to produce and distribute something successfully. So the production cost has to be multiplied three times to get to the selling price, so as to cover the costs of:

◆ **Marketing**, to bring the publication to the attention of potential readers (purchasers), where you may produce a catalogue or a leaflet advertising the publication, and will need to spend money on mailing this out and on other forms of promotion, including free copies sent out for review.

◆ **Distribution**, getting the publication to the purchaser, which involves the cost of storage, handling the order, the postage and the packing, handling and accounting for the money. It may also include offering a discount for those taking copies of the publication to re-sell. If you can offer a reasonable discount (usually between 30% and 35%) to bookshops and other voluntary organisations, then you will find that they are happy to sell your publication. There will also be the costs of unsaleable stock, including stock surplus to requirements and damaged returns and cases of invoiced sales where the purchaser does not pay.

So if you print 1,000 copies of a booklet at a total cost of Rs 12,000, the selling price using this formula would be Rs 12 per copy x 3 = Rs 36, which you may then want to adjust by rounding up or down, in this case to Rs 35.

But there are two points to bear in mind while deciding the price of your publication to make it commercially viable:

◆ **Costs should be kept as low as possible** and consistent with an acceptable level of quality. People are not prepared to pay high prices for publications, and the primary objective in producing your publication is to get the information out to people. You will find that costs can be reduced through careful design, printing in just one or two colours, choosing good value paper, and by careful selection of a printer.

◆ If you price the publication, you can always decide that **some people receive it free** or have **differential subscription rates** (higher for overseas subscribers, government and business, and lower for voluntary organisations). And if the publication is not selling well, say by the end of the first year, you might then decide to put more effort into marketing it or have a 'special offer' or start sending it out free simply to get it out of your office and into people's hands.

Examples of pricing strategies

Many voluntary organisations producing publications put a 10% mark up on costs. This is what Multiple Action Research Group (MARG) does, for example, with its legal literacy publications.

This mark up does not allow them enough to pay for any additional marketing or to offer a discount to distributors and bookshops, with the result that there can be little active marketing, and MARG has to wait for orders to come in rather than create a demand. A more commercial approach to pricing would solve this, and better marketing could mean longer print runs and lower unit costs.

SEARCH, a training and development organisation based in Bangalore, publishes the quarterly *SEARCH Bulletin*. This was distributed free to a mailing list of 3,000 people. SEARCH decided to move from free distribution to paid subscription. At a price of Rs 150 per annum. When it launched its subscription scheme, it gave recipients two issues to decide to pay. The circulation decreased to just around 650. SEARCH was pleased with this. It now had a core readership that wanted the publication (SEARCH had never been certain who read it and who did not); it could still print 3,000 copies, but use the extra 2,350 copies to get new subscribers and for special promotions linked to the theme of the particular issue; some income was now being generated.

Developing a fundraising strategy

In the first chapter, we examined some of the reasons for wanting to fundraise, and suggested how you might use these to create a **mission statement** for your fundraising. This will provide you with a framework for developing your fundraising, and you will be able to select fundraising methods according to how they help you achieve your 'fundraising mission'.

The other important factor you need to consider is **how much do you need to raise**. You need to take into account the following:

◆ Your **existing budget;** how much you are spending; how much income has been raised towards future expenditure and how much is to be arranged.

◆ The amount you **currently raise** from Indian and local sources, and any **fundraising experience** you have.

◆ Your organisation's **future growth** and development.

◆ **Confidence** in your abilities (as an organisation and in yourself who will be responsible for the fundraising) to raise money you need.

◆ The **opportunities** that exist for raising money, and the chances of success. You may be lucky; there may be something that you can do that will generate a great deal of money without too much risk. On the other hand (and this is much more likely), you may have to work hard to raise small amounts.

Starting up in fundraising is difficult. You have to develop your contacts, your expertise in the techniques you plan to use and suitable materials. Do not lose heart as you will learn from experience—fundraising becomes easier over time. But remember that it takes time, and things will happen more slowly than you think.

A step-by-step guide to developing a strategy

Step 1   Deciding your strategy

You must have a **strategy** (that will give a **focus** to what you are doing) and **targets** (that will set **goals** to be achieved). It is better to be realistic and set targets that stand a chance of being achieved, than to be over-optimistic. If you are more successful than you thought you would be, then this will raise your confidence and you can always increase the scale of your target as you go along in the light of your experience and success. This is better than having targets that are too high, and being disappointed, which might lead to a financial crisis.

There are two things you need to decide:

◆ **How much** will you raise? You should set targets for what you will raise over the next three years. This should represent an increasing proportion of your total expenditure each year.

◆ **How** will you raise the money?

If you are starting from scratch, it may be sensible to set a target of about 10% of total expenditure being raised from individuals, companies and events after two to three years. If you already have some experience, 20% to 25% might be an achievable target. What target you set will also depend on the size of your organisation and the scale of its activities.

TO DO   **Set targets for how much to raise**

What proportion of your current budget do you think you can manage to generate through fundraising:

Next year:	.........%	Rs ....
The year after:	.........%	Rs ....
In 3 years' time:	.........%	Rs ....

Step 2   Deciding how you will raise the money. Making a plan

In *Chapter 4*, we looked at some of the fundraising techniques that you can use to raise money. You now need to decide, which of these you will concentrate on, as it is not sensible to try too many things at once.

CHECKLIST Where will you get the money?

These are the main sources of money. Think about which you will concentrate on:

- **From individuals**
- ☐ Getting support from **individual donors** who are interested in your work through membership or donations. Building a **mailing list**.
- ☐ Getting support from the **local community** where your project is based.
- ☐ Raising money through **fundraising events** such as public collections, entertainment events and participation events (such as sponsored walks).
- ☐ Asking individuals to give their time (as **volunteers**).
- ☐ Getting support through your **overseas contacts** and setting up overseas support groups.
- ☐ Finding creative ways of raising support from **tourists and tourism**.

- **From companies, foundations and donor agencies**
- ☐ A grant from an **international source** or a **foundation** (or similar grant-making bodies).
- ☐ Getting **cash** support from companies.
- ☐ Getting support from companies through **sponsorship**.
- ☐ Getting **support in kind** (from individuals as well as from companies); donations of products and services.
- ☐ Getting support from companies through donation of **skills, expertise or facilities**.

- **From government sources**
- ☐ A grant from a **central government department** (including grants from government-sponsored agencies such as Council for Advancement of People's Action and Rural Technology (CAPART).
- ☐ A grant from a **local government source** (village or panchayat, town or city, district or state).

- **From earned income**
- ☐ Income generated through **fees, charges** and sales of **information and expertise**.
- ☐ Sales of **greetings cards**.
- ☐ Sales of **craft items and other products** made in the course of your development work.

Do two things:

1. From which of these sources do you see yourself raising money? Use the tick boxes to note which you think are possibilities. Think through whether you really want to be using this method.
2. List your selection of sources in some sort of priority order.

Remember the following:

1. **Do not attempt too many different fundraising activities all at once**. It is best to concentrate on just a few, and do them well, no more than three (or four at the most) in the first instance.

2. **Assess the relevance of each to your fundraising strategy**. Thinking about this might prompt you not to undertake a particular activity, or even to consider something that you have not listed. For example, if an important part of your strategy is to create an active group of supporters, then approaching rich individuals for large donations would not really meet your strategic objectives.

3. **Think about your capability** of raising money through each method. You should concentrate on what you think you will be best at.

For most organisations starting up in fundraising, the following will be appropriate:

◆   To build up a **supporter list** or develop a **membership scheme**.

◆   To raise money from the **local community**.

◆   To organise **one fundraising event** each year.

◆   To raise **support from business** (in cash and in kind, or through sponsorship).

◆   To seek out opportunities that may exist, for raising money from **tourists, returning volunteers or overseas contacts**.

Some of these you can do on a planned basis. Some when the opportunity occurs.

4. For each of these activities, identify the key steps that need to be taken to get started, including the resources you will require and the next steps that you will take to start to implement the fundraising activity. This will then form the basis of an action plan.

5. You should now prepare a paper, setting out your fundraising strategy and your plans, with reasons for having suggested these.

TO DO   Developing and presenting a plan

First, develop a fundraising plan for your organisation. Then...

Prepare a presentation of not more than 10 minutes setting out the proposed strategy and targets, the feasibility, the problem areas and the steps you propose to take thereafter.

Step 3   Getting your strategy and plans approved

You will need the approval of the Board for your fundraising strategy, including their agreement for the fundraising strategy paper you have presented. In particular, you will need to get their agreement to the following:

◆ The fundraising **mission statement**, which gives the reasons for doing the fundraising.

◆ The **fundraising methods** you have planned to use.

◆ The **targets**.

◆ Any **donations policy** you have drawn up, which sets out who you are not prepared to accept support from (*see section* 'Ethics and accountability' *on page 28*).

◆ The **resource implications** (*see below*), and a **budget** that will enable you to implement your plans.

As part of your presentation to the Board, it can be helpful to mention, what other organisations are doing? These could be 'rival' organisations doing similar work, as well as some of the more important organisations of a similar standing to your own. If you can show examples of successful fundraising by these organisations, it may make it easier to persuade your Board.

Step 4   Clarifying the constraints

There will always be a number of constraints on what you can do. Some stem from the nature of the organisation and what it stands for. Some are internally generated. Some are externally imposed. However they arise, you need to take them into account when you are planning your fundraising.

◆ **Are there any legal constraints?** Are you able to receive foreign funds? Are you registered as a charitable organisation so that you can receive tax exempt donations? Will gift tax be payable? There are a whole range of legal and taxation issues that need to be considered. Some will determine, who you can receive funds from, others will ensure that you get the best tax advantage from any support you receive. All this needs to be understood and sorted out before you start (*see section* 'Legal and tax matters' *on page 15*).

◆ **Are your interests national, or purely local?** Are you a national or a local organisation? And if you are local, is what you are doing of national significance or importance? Most national and international funding sources will want to support national projects or what they consider to be the best local projects— work that is innovative or at the leading edge. They are unlikely to respond to requests from local projects they have never heard of.

Local sources will usually only support local projects that are operating in the area. Local people will certainly be more interested in supporting projects at their doorstep. And companies will only want to support local projects in those areas where they have a business presence or some business connection or where they are planning to start up.

◆ **Are there any 'no go' areas?** The ethical problems of fundraising have been discussed in the section 'Ethics and accountability', when we suggested that you need to have a donations policy that sets out what kinds of donations you are **not prepared to accept** on ethical grounds, and that you need to have this policy agreed to by the Board.

◆ **Are you aware of the attractiveness of the cause?** You need to think about whether your cause is instantly attractive to donors (helping street children is; working with leprosy patients much less so). If your cause is attractive, then you will find it easier to get individuals to support you. If it is not immediately attractive, then you will have to find ways of making it seem so.

If you are a radical and campaigning organisation, you will find that, those who share your views are prepared to support you, but those who do not, will not. Most companies and many 'establishment' sources will not want to support anything that is 'too political' or too controversial, and will prefer to support activities that are safe and conservative. This can impose a constraint on who to approach.

◆ **The scale of your need**. If you need large amounts of money, there is no point approaching someone who can only give a little—unless you are planning a major campaign where you intend to recruit large numbers of small donors. Nor is it sensible to spend a lot of time organising a fundraising event which could only generate a small sum. Equally, if you are just looking for some modest support, there is no point approaching a huge international foundation.

Step 5   What resources are available to you?

The resources available to you determine what you can and what you can not do. You will need to decide whether you have:

◆ The **people** to organise the activity. Will **you** do it? Will someone else do it? Can you find people to do it? Will they be paid? Or will you use volunteers?

◆ The **skills and experience** you will need. What do you plan to do, and what skills are needed to do this? Do you have these skills? Or, can you get them?

◆ The **information** you require on those potential sources of support you plan to approach. This is critical for approaching companies and foundations. What information do you have? What will you need to get? How will you do this?

◆ **Contacts** with prominent people who you can use in your fundraising. If you are approaching companies, it helps to have senior business people who are prepared to help you ask. A request from them is much more likely to be successful. If you are organising an event, having a **star personality** who is prepared to attend or participate will also increase the likelihood of success.

◆ Your **credibility** as an organisation, and the importance and value of your work. People want to be associated only with important, successful organisations (whether local, or national). Will they want to be associated with you? What can you do *(a)* to boost your organisation's credibility? And *(b)* to communicate this to the people that you want support from? Getting good publicity for your work, obtaining endorsements and having stories of success will all help. The chapter on 'Communicating the work of your organisation' discusses the communications skills you will need. If you have done an evaluation, then this can provide evidence that what you are doing is successful, and provide information for donors on how effective you have been.

◆ **Time**. This includes the time available for organising, running and administering the proposed fundraising activity or activities. But it also includes having sufficient preparation time to organise the particular activity, as many will require months to plan and organise.

Raising funds for your fundraising

There are basically three approaches to raising the income for your fundraising strategy, which you could combine:

1. Start with almost nothing

It does not cost much money to send out 50 or even 500 letters. Many organisations have begun in this way. The Association of Persons with Disability (APD) began by writing to 60 friends; Lok Kalyan Samiti (LKS) began by writing to 350 people getting the addresses from a neighbourhood directory.

2. Find the money within your existing budget

If you believe that establishing a fundraising programme is vital because without public support and donations it may be very difficult, if not impossible, to continue, then try to find money within your existing budget. This could be within your agreed budget allocations (for publicity and communication, for example). Or it might involve a reallocation, when you might need to get the agreement of your existing funders. This is what Jeevika, a voluntary organisation in Karnataka, working to release children from bonded labour, has done.

3. Raise funds specially for your fundraising programme

You can do this by approaching a grant-making agency, which is sympathetic to you or, which is currently supporting you. Association for Leprosy Education, Rehabilitation and Treatment (ALERT), an organisation based in Mumbai, was in a very difficult financial situation in 1992 because of the sudden withdrawal of funds by a foreign donor agency. They asked Oxfam (because Oxfam had supported them in earlier days) for funds to begin a fundraising programme. ALERT was given a grant of Rs 300,000 for this purpose, which it used to get going in fundraising. ALERT now raises Rs 3,500,000 from within India each year for its work.

There is a general principle that can be stated: 'It costs money to raise money'. And if you are serious about getting started in fundraising, then you will have to find the resources to make a start.

◆ The **money to invest** in the activity. It is possible to get started with very little, or even nothing. But you may need to invest money up front to produce literature, undertake promotion and/or organise an event. What do you need to spend money on? How much money is required? You should prepare a budget alongside your fundraising plan. It can be quite modest. And for those who are starting out, it is best to start slowly, spending as little as you can get away with. Is your Board prepared to make this budget available to you? What are the chances of raising more than you are planning to spend? Are there things you can do to reduce the risk or guarantee a return?

◆ **Training, networking and support**. Do you need training? What training opportunities exist? Will these (check first, as not all fundraising training is relevant to small organisations starting up) be useful? What networks exist for sharing ideas and experiences with others doing similar fundraising work?

Step 6   Deciding who will do the work, and who will be responsible for it

Your fundraising will only work if someone is made responsible for 'delivering the goods' and is given appropriate time and resources to do the work effectively, and if there is an appropriate management and decision structure. This will require:

◆ A **plan and a budget** that is agreed upon.

◆ A member of staff to be put **in charge** of the fundraising (that is probably you!).

◆ A **line management structure** for that member of staff to report to (unless the person in charge is the Chief Executive). The fundraiser should report, if possible, directly to the Chief Executive for two reasons. First, many fundraising proposals have implications for the work of the organisation, and what you ask money for needs to be agreed to, before you ask. Second, the Chief Executive will be required from time to time to attend important fundraising meetings. If you are approaching a major donor agency, a senior Director of a large company or an extremely wealthy person, then they will respond better if someone from the top level of the organisation approaches them.

◆ A **Board Member** should be given the responsibility of overseeing the activities at the Board level. Perhaps a separate **Fundraising and Development Committee** could be created to bring together people with interest in developing the resource base of the organisation and with skills and experience to provide advice and support to the staff.

◆ A **support structure**, for you to discuss progress/problems and share your ideas. A small group of people – comprising one or two people from the Board, one or two staff (including the one responsible for public relations), and one or two outsiders who have a useful perspective or experience – could form a fundraising support group for you.

◆ **Professional advice**. You may find you need help with organising a direct mail campaign, producing promotional literature or doing the public relations. If you do not have the skills and there is nobody in-house to do the work, then you will need to look outside. This may cost, but you may find that you can persuade someone to do it for free.

A suggested plan of action for the first year

Month 1:

1. The persons responsible should try to **meet others** who are doing some fundraising... to learn as much as they can.

2. Prepare a 12-month **detailed plan of action**. This will have dates for dispatch of appeals, newsletters, the annual report and an annual fundraising 'week' for the organisation.

Month 2:

3. Collect **addresses** of friends and well-wishers, and prepare receipt books for all donations you will receive. Store the addresses on 5" x 3" cards, or in a computer file, in an organised way.

Month 3:

4. Prepare the first **warm appeal letter** to be sent to friends and well-wishers. Take trouble on this; modify, rework, improve, finalise and then print to the quantity you have decided. Send it out.

5. Make contact with **the media**, especially with local newspapers and magazines and begin to obtain press coverage for your work and the issues you are addressing.

Months 4–6:

6. Hold a **planning meeting** for the annual 'week' (or 'month'). Plan one large event with an emphasis on 'raising awareness' for your organisation and its work, and one or two smaller events with an emphasis on fundraising.

7. Find suitable addresses to send your mailing to. Dispatch first **cold appeal letters**. Acknowledge all replies promptly with a thank you letter and a formal receipt.

Months 7–8:

8. Organise the **annual fundraising week** to get publicity and raise awareness.

Months 9–10:

9. Prepare an A4 size two-page or four-page **newsletter**. Send this out to all donors and contacts.

10. Organise the two smaller **fundraising events**.

Month 12:

11. **Evaluate progress** during your first year.

12. Draw up **plans for the next two years**.

Doing a SWOT analysis

A SWOT analysis identifies the **strengths, weaknesses, opportunities** and the **threats** to the organisation. By doing a SWOT analysis for your fundraising, you will be able to develop:

◆ fundraising strategies, methods and activities, which **build on your strengths**;

◆ avoid those **areas of weakness** or find ways of compensating them;

◆ seize the **opportunities** that present themselves;

◆ develop ways of **dealing with the threats** that appear on the horizon (such as the loss of a grant).

Here are some examples of strengths, weaknesses, opportunities and threats that a SWOT analysis might generate:

◆ **Strengths**

An active group of volunteers.

Good contacts with local industrialists or a major company.

A well-respected and long-established organisation.

An active group of volunteers who are happy to run fundraising events for you.

◆ **Weaknesses**

No existing fundraising experience.

No obvious person to do the work.

Poor promotional material.

Being very new; not having much of a track record.

◆ **Opportunities**

A major company has just moved in your area.

A new government funding programme has just been announced.

Your 25th anniversary.

A TV documentary or newspaper article on your work is about to go out.

Your base is in the middle of an extremely affluent community.

A consultant will do free training for you.

◆ **Threats**

Structural adjustment will lead to price rises, which will affect potential supporters.

You are in confrontation with the government, which leads to adverse publicity.

> ## TO DO SWOT analysis
>
> Do a SWOT analysis, identifying the strengths, weaknesses, opportunities and the threats to the organisation and its fundraising programmes.
>
> - **Strengths**
> - **Weaknesses**
> - **Opportunities**
> - **Threats**

How to write a fundraising proposal

Writing a good fundraising proposal is probably one of the most important skills you will need if you are to make a success of your fundraising. A proposal sets out what you want to do. Its function is to persuade people to support you.

There is no one way of writing a good proposal. The advice that follows should not be regarded as a blueprint which will guarantee success. What it aims to do is to help you understand the key points so that you are able to produce a proposal which stands a better chance of being successful.

The same basic principles apply when approaching:

◆   a grant-making body;

◆   a company;

◆   an individual.

Where differences exist, these are identified in the text.

What to ask for

One of the key skills is to decide what to ask for. Most donors are:

◆   Interested in **projects**, rather than supporting the core costs of running the organisation.

◆   Interested in projects that **catch their imagination**, because they seem lively, interesting or innovative, and which match their own policies and priorities.

◆   Interested in projects that are of **the size that they are happy to support** (whether they are being asked to provide all of the costs or just a proportion).

Even where you are raising money for work that you have been doing for many years, it is possible to 'package' it as a project and present it in an interesting way. If you can do this, you will vastly improve your chances of success. This is an important fundraising skill, and there is a separate section giving advice on 'Raising Money for a Project'.

Planning your approach

In thinking about how to structure a proposal, you will need to consider the following:

◆ **Who** will you be asking?

◆ What are **their priorities and interests**?

◆ How are you going to **contact** them?

◆ What **procedure** do they have for assessing grant applications and making decisions on grants?

◆ What **information** will you need to write the proposal—and how much will you need to say about yourself and what you propose to do? And...

◆ How and by when, do you have to **submit the application**?

There are several factors to consider at this stage:

◆ **Application forms**. You should find out from the donor whether the application needs to be submitted in any standard format, or if there is an application form that you could use. When completing an application form, make sure that you read the guidance to applicants extremely carefully, noting the key points so that you answer all the questions fully and carefully.

◆ **How many donors do you plan to approach**? For individuals and companies, you may be sending the proposal to a number of donors. You should try to make it personal to each. The simplest way of doing this is by having a standard proposal, which provides all the information that is needed about the project or programme and accompanied by a short covering letter. This will tell the donor why you are approaching them, why they should support you and how much you would like them to give? When approaching major donors, it is best to select just one or two, where you feel there is a real chance of success, and to make the proposal personal to them and their particular priorities and interests.

◆ **Size of the donor**. Large donor bodies (which include international donor agencies, major foundations and the government) will be interested in a great deal of detail. They are looking not just for good ideas, but also for evidence of necessity of the project and professionalism in your work. Smaller donors (which include companies and most individuals) just do not have the time to read through a mountain of paper. Keep your proposal to them short and simple (this is known as the 'KISS principle').

◆ **The likely outcome**. Larger the grant applied for and greater the likelihood of success, the more it is worth putting time and effort into your application. Conversely, for smaller amounts or where your chances are low, you should limit the time you put into writing the proposal if you are to be cost-effective. It is a general principle of fundraising that it is better to put more effort into fewer things that are likely to succeed, than to scatter your efforts widely where there is less chance of success.

Content of the proposal

You have to make a good case. You should try to answer a series of questions, which the donor will expect answers to, before deciding to support you. You should also have a logical structure for the proposal. The following will provide you with a framework for making your case:

Section 1: Summary

Very long proposals (10 pages or more) should contain a one-page summary at the start. For short proposals, this is not necessary. Proposals of between three and nine pages might contain a short summary (perhaps two paragraphs) as an introductory section. This allows busy people to see at a glance, what you are proposing and to decide whether it is relevant to them and whether they should read on.

Section 2: Introducing yourself

Here you state briefly who you are, what you do, how you work and why you are well qualified to carry out the work you are proposing.

You might want to back this up with more detailed information in an accompanying leaflet or an appendix. For applications to major donors, you might provide the following: Curriculum vitae of the key organisers and others involved; where you have a well-connected committee or patrons, a list of their names; evidence of support you have previously received from other major donors or a government body. If you have had press coverage, you can include photocopies of the clippings. If you have had a major evaluation done on your work, then that might be worth summarising. If you have received feedback from users, experts or others, then you can mention this or provide an analysis of the response you've had or include a direct quote.

It is useful to have some key details of your organisation on your letterhead—date founded, registration details, names of board members and patrons.

Section 3: Setting out the problem

◆ What is the **problem** or the **need** that is to be met? You should consider the scale of the need, whether things are getting better or worse. If the problem itself is not widely recognised, references to other respected reports or endorsements by prominent people will help, along with facts and figures from your own or other people's research.

◆ Are there any particular **geographic or socio-economic factors** that make it important to do something in the area and with the people you plan to work with? Many donors like to support projects that work with the poorest and the most disadvantaged, and they do not want their work to duplicate what is already being done. Can you provide the facts to show this?

Section 4: Stating what you plan to do

At the heart of your proposal, you will describe the aims of your project, and how you will achieve them. You should include as much detail as is necessary for a person who is not knowledgeable in your area.

◆ What are the **aims** of your project?

◆ What **working methods** will be used to meet these aims? You will need to describe these in much more detail in an application for a large project.

◆ What are your **short- and long-term operational plans**? What is the programme of work that you are planning?

◆ Will you have the support of **the local community**, and how will they be involved?

◆ Will you be **collaborating with other organisations**, which will bring in additional skills and resources?

◆ Will you be able to mobilise the **efforts and energies of volunteers**, and how much value will this add to the work being done?

◆ How will you be dealing with some of the **key issues** that concern them, things such as: gender, participatory techniques, capacity building of the local community, rights and advocacy work, etc.? This is relevant usually only when applying to major donors.

◆ If the work is innovative, what plans do you have for **dissemination**? And is it possible that your success will influence how others address the problem?

Section 5: Saying how you will measure success

You should also give an indication as to how you would expect to measure the successful outcome of the project.

◆ What are the **expected outcomes and achievements**? You should set clear and measurable objectives for the project.

◆ You should describe how you will **monitor progress and evaluate success**. This should relate to the objectives you have set. For a large project, there might be an external evaluation.

Section 6: Stating how much you will need

You need to have a clear **budget** for the work, and be able to **justify all the expenditure**. For large projects, this can be set out in detail. For smaller proposals, a summary of income and expenditure is all that you will need.

Your budget will always be carefully scrutinised by potential funders, and needs to be clear, complete and accurate. Most donors will not be interested in the small details of your stationery or postage bills. What they will be interested in are the major areas of expenditure and income.

Advice on how to budget for projects is given in a separate section on *'Raising Money for Projects'*.

Section 7: Saying how you plan to raise the money

Your budget will show how much you need to raise. Here you show how you are going to raise it:

◆ What **sources of funds** have you already identified? And what commitment have you already made to the project?

◆ What do you want as a **contribution from the donor** you are approaching, and for how many years (a one-off donation or continuing support for three or five years)?

◆ **When** do you need the money?

Section 8: Looking at what is going to happen in the future

Most donors are concerned about sustainability. They want to know what will happen when the grant comes to an end:

◆ Will the project be able to continue on a self-sustainable basis? Or...

◆ Will you be able to identify and develop alternative sources of funding to support it? Or...

◆ Will the project come to a natural end?

Donors like to see their support as an investment, which will continue to bring benefits into the future. They don't want to feel that they are locked into supporting you for ever. They want you to think about the future, even if you cannot develop any firm plans at present.

Section 9: Telling them why they might be interested

It's always a good idea to try to **relate your proposal to their interests and priorities**, to show how well it fits in with these and how it provides an opportunity to take forward their own agenda or programme.

When **approaching companies**, an additional factor to consider is, what you can offer **in return** to the company. For most companies this will be an important consideration, and for any sponsorship proposal it is crucial. Things to consider are:

◆ Ways in which you can **publicise the company's support** (in your annual reports, newsletters, the local press, etc.) and the number of people that will become aware of the company's support.

◆ For a sponsorship, ways in which you can get **publicity for the company's products or services**.

◆ The interest and involvement of the company's own **employees** in your organisation as fundraisers or volunteers (many companies like to support what their employees are involved with).

◆ The proximity of your organisation to any **major location** or factory of the company, as the company will be happy if it is seen as being socially responsible and a good citizen among the community it operates with.

Section 10: Additional information

When you are approaching a company or a major donor agency, you will almost certainly need to supply your organisation's audited accounts for the past one to three years. For an individual, you can attach a leaflet explaining your organisation's work or showing case studies. Very large applications may require a lot of additional information included as an appendix.

How much to ask for

You will try to find out the size of grant that the particular donor usually makes, during your preliminary research. Some donors will provide you with a list of grants they have made over the year; or you can ask them what range of grants they normally make, whether they make one-off grants or give regular support over a certain number of years, and the size of grant that you might apply for.

You may realise that they are giving less than the total you need to raise. In such a case, you will need to approach more than one donor, asking each to contribute a part of the total. There are several approaches to this:

◆ **The total sum is shared between a number of donors**: You can approach, say, three different sources, and ask each to contribute one-third of the total (or an appropriate proportion, depending on their size).

◆ **Each donor is asked to support a particular aspect of your work**: You can break down the project into separate components. For a capital project, this might include:

    Land purchase

    Basic building work

    Equipping the building

    Marketing the project

    Getting started (the running costs for the first year while it gets going)

    Producing a report of the project

    Dissemination (perhaps organising a conference to launch the project)

Each of these might become the subject of an application to a particular donor, and you would provide a separate budget for that item. In each application, you would highlight the particular importance of what you are asking that donor to support—as well as the value of the project as a whole.

Then there is the question of strategy. Do you approach all your prospective donors at the same time? Or do you approach one of them first, hoping to gain their support, before approaching the others? This is something only you can decide. If you have a donor with whom you have worked closely in the past and who is prepared to make a commitment to support the project, then that fact might encourage others. On the other hand, if you have to wait to get a commitment from one donor before approaching others, then that can delay the funding process. Whatever you decide, it is important to have a funding plan, and to explain to everyone you approach how you propose to raise all of the money you need.

TO DO   What are the key points you want to make in your proposal?

As an exercise before you start writing your proposal, make a list of **all the key points** you need to make—perhaps there will be six really important points, perhaps more. But remember, too much information will make the application less powerful.

Writing skills

When writing up your proposal there are several factors to consider:

◆ **Length**: There is a lot of information you could put in. If you put it all in, your application would be too long for many funders. If you are looking for a very substantial grant, then a very long application may be appropriate. For less complicated and smaller proposals, keep the length to a minimum. A page or at most two pages will normally be sufficient when you are looking for support from a company or an individual. You can always attach more detailed information as an appendix or include a photograph or technical information related to the proposal—if you feel that it could be of interest to the donor.

◆ **Language and jargon**: Many applications are extremely badly written and boring to read. If you have the skill to do so, try to write the application in a lively upbeat way. Things to avoid are; long words, long sentences, long paragraphs, meaningless words and jargon, and waffle. It is far better to have:

> **Shorter words**, rather than long words.
>
> **Shorter sentences**, rather than long sentences.
>
> **Shorter paragraphs**, rather than long paragraphs.
>
> **Bullet points and lists** of key points, rather than continuous sentences (when appropriate).

Bold or in *italics* to highlight key features.

Headings and **subheadings** to indicate the different parts of the application.

The best advice is to get someone to read what you have written before you send it off and the best person is someone who knows only a little about your work, as that is the position of most of the people you will be sending your application to. They can ask for explanations and challenge assumptions where things seem unclear to them.

◆ **Facts and figures**: It is important to backup your claims – about the extent of the need and the effectiveness of your methods – with facts and figures, rather than talk in generalities. Everything may be **desperate, urgent, important, unique**; but you need to **prove** this by stating facts. Try to include a few selected facts and figures in your proposal. You can, if you want, also provide a wealth of detail in a background paper attached as an appendix to the application.

◆ **The human story**: If you can include case studies and examples of how people have been helped and what they have gone on to achieve as a result of your help, then this will demonstrate clearly that you are effective in helping people— which is what most donors are interested in supporting. This can be done within the proposal, or as an appendix or in an accompanying leaflet. *See the separate section on* 'Using Case Studies', *page 138*.

◆ **Presentation**: How you present your proposal is luckily not the most important aspect, but it can make a difference. Different standards and expectations apply to different donors. A sponsorship proposal directed at the Marketing Director of a major company will have to have a different feel to a proposal being sent to a national foundation that receives dozens of proposals each day. And government agencies and international donors will have their own standards and preferred styles. Remember to tailor your style of communication to whoever it is you are dealing with.

Timing

It always takes longer than you think to prepare a proposal; you should allow yourself at least a month, if you have not fully formulated your thoughts or if you need to consult others, for the proposal. There will often be a good deal of information to be collected, which could take time. And after the first draft, careful editing has to be done, and a perfectly typed final copy produced.

There is the application procedure of the funder to be considered. Some major donors only process applications once a year. A large company may consider appeals on a quarterly or even a monthly basis, and may be able to respond to an emergency immediately—although it may have spent the whole of its budget for the year when you applied. An individual will respond when approached, but certain times of the year may be better than others (holiday season, the end of the tax year, for example).

Appeal Letter from 'Happy Childhoods' to Azharuddin and Tendulkar, two famous Indian cricketers, asking for support

This letter was written by Shikha Ghildyal of Save the Children Fund for a competition at the 1997 South Asian Fundraising Workshop. Participants were asked to write to these two cricketers proposing that they contribute their appearance fees for the Sahara Cup in Toronto to create some 'good luck' for the Indian cricket team after a less than satisfactory performance in Sri Lanka. This letter won the first prize. It deserved to. It is extremely well written. Happy Childhoods is a fictitious organisation.

Dear Mr Azharuddin and Mr Tendulkar

Before I commence with the appeal I am going to make to you for funding a project for the organisation I represent, let me say how much I admire you both and how honoured I feel to be writing to people who work so hard to serve our country.

They say that 'childhood is the best time of one's life'. But how many children in our country can say that today? My organisation, called Happy Childhoods, works towards making this a reality for as many children as possible.

The project for which I am requesting money is for children who have no 'childhood' because their little shoulders carry the burden of adulthood. They have learnt to cry before knowing laughter and to work without knowing rest, and will continue to do so unless people like you intervene. These are the children whose little hands work late into the night—every night—without holding a ball to play or a pen to write. They work in inhuman conditions, because if they don't, they will die of hunger or cold—at the same time knowing in their hearts that if they continue to work like this, they will die anyway.

There are millions of children in India involved in child labour, and try as we might, we cannot protect all of them. Our endeavour has been to raise funds from the very people for whom these children labour, and to use that money to educate, feed and bring some laughter and sunshine through play into their darkened, hopeless lives.

Till now, we have collected money from women who wear bangles for children who work in glass factories, from smokers for children who work in the *beedi* (local cigarette) industry—and from you, Sir, we hope to raise money for the children whose tiny hands stitch the cricket balls without which there would be no cricket and no cricket team.

The Rs 500,000 that we are asking you to give will mean and achieve far less than the fact that the very people for whom the balls are being made are the ones who show they care!

The money will be put towards providing education for children working in the cricket ball industry in Jullundur. It will teach the children not only to write their names, but also to read yours in the newspaper, and share your victories as if they were their own. It will help build on earth, 'castles that were in the air'. We hope that we will be able to utilise this money so well that the next appeal you receive for funds will not be from our organisation.

We promise that every rupee you give us will go towards putting a smile on a child's face and stars in their eyes and a hope and a prayer in their voice to carry you through 'centuries' of success. Help us give these children the childhood they deserve.

Yours sincerely...

Now think about why this letter is so good and whether you could write something as good. Read it with a group of friends and discuss (and learn from it).

Improving your writing skills

Many people are unable to write in a lively and interesting way. This requires skills, which you can usually learn and improve through practice.

Here are some worked examples to show how you can improve the quality of your writing... and the impact of your proposal.

Actual example 1. The question as to whether the organisation has been fully transparent and accountable in its use of resources has yet to be addressed by the Management Committee, but the matter is being given some priority at the present time.

Improved version: 'We make every effort to use our resources effectively and to keep donors informed about our work.'

Comment: The words 'transparent' and 'accountable' are jargon. Explain what you mean simply. And use the first person (we) not the third person (the organisation). This last point applies also to most of the following examples.

Actual example 2. On numerous occasions, the organisation has met with government officials to seek a resolution to the problems. But each time it was felt that progress had been made, it proved impossible to extract from government officials any realistic timetable for the implementation of what the organisation thought had been agreed to, with the consequence that absolutely no progress has been made on this score, and the problems seem set to continue for the indefinite future.

Improved version: 'We have had many meetings with Government where we felt we had reached an agreement on what needed to be done and a timetable for dealing with the problem. But we have had no success in getting Government officials to implement what they had agreed to. Unless we find a way around this, the problem seems set to continue.'

Comment: Think about what you actually want to say. Then say it!

Actual example 3. A large number of meetings were organised in project villages where the participants interacted on women's awareness, identification of women's problems, their potentiality and participation in village development, the dowry evil, oppression in family as well as in society, income generation initiatives and economic self-reliance.

Improved version: 'We have organised a large number of meetings for women in the villages, where we have sought to:

* *Increase their awareness of problems in their lives and possible solutions.*

* *Encourage their participation in village development.*

* *Discuss the issues of dowry, violence and other factors that oppress them.*

* *Develop ideas for income-generation activities that will lead to greater economic self-reliance.'*

Comment: Use 'bullet points'. This makes things clearer.

Getting in touch

Finding out as much as you can before you make the approach is important. These are the things you need to know:

- The **donations policy** of the **geographical and programme focus** of their grant making. There is no point applying for something that they cannot or will not support.

- The sort of things they have **supported in the past**—so that you know their interests and the size of grant they are likely to make, and can tailor your approach accordingly.

- **Who to write to** (their name and job title), but also **who makes the decisions** and who they are advised by (so you can plan any lobbying).

- Whether they expect to get any sort of **recognition or benefit in return** for their support. Think about this when you plan your proposal.

- Their **decision-making cycle** and the best time for applications to be submitted.

The following will help you in deciding the above:

- **Research** the donors you plan to approach, bringing together information from a variety of sources, and keep this information on record. A card index or computer file can be used.

- **Telephone** and find out the contact person and application procedure.

- **Suggest a meeting** or invite the prospective donor to visit your project.

- **Find out as much as you can** about their detailed decision-making process by asking the donor, and by talking to others who have received support from that donor.

- Contact any **key advisor or trustee** of the donor organisation to tell them about your proposal, if you can get access to either.

- Write a **draft proposal**, personalised as much as possible to the needs of the donor, seek comments on this from colleagues and then redraft. If you have a good relationship with the donor, you can send them the draft, and ask if it is along the right lines, before submitting your final proposal.

- Produce and send off the **final application**, together with appended information to provide details.

Persistence

A key skill in fundraising is persistence. If someone says *'No'*, think about how to get them to say *'Yes'* next time around... or the next next time around.

Nine Dos and Six Don'ts for writing a proposal

1. DO address your appeal to **the right person**, with name and job title correctly spelt.
2. DO **tailor your appeal** to the interests and concerns of the recipient.
3. DO include a clear statement of your organisation's **objectives and work**.
4. DO state clearly **the purpose** for which the funds are needed and the amount required.
5. DO break a large appeal into **manageable, realistic amounts** for different donors.
6. DO include **your latest annual accounts**.
7. DO offer to go and **see the prospective donor**, and follow up with a letter within a week.
8. DO make full use of any **contacts** you have who might be prepared to introduce you to the donor.
9. DO **keep it brief**.

1. DON'T make your appeal letter look **mass-produced**.
2. DON'T include **irrelevant information** or large quantities of printed material.
3. DON'T get **angry at a refusal**—nobody can support every request.
4. DON'T be **put off by a refusal**—try again next year.
5. DON'T feel obliged to **offer expensive hospitality** to a prospective donor.
6. DON'T give **too little time for the response**—it could take months for a decision to be made.

TO DO   Write a letter asking for support

As an exercise in improving your proposal writing skills, choose one of these scenarios:

Scenario 1

You have a mailing list of 100 individuals who have already supported you in some way, and are now going to write to a further 2,500 people from appropriate lists you have been able to acquire.

Scenario 2

You plan to write to 50 leading companies asking them for support.

Your task is to write a letter to ask for support using some of the principles enunciated here. You should do this in 350 to 700 words, and in plain language that the donor can understand.

The letter you send will be accompanied by a leaflet that can explain things in more detail—include pictures of your project and people being helped.

You have identified them as potentially interested in your work. You have failed to get them to support you this time. But there is always a next time. How can you do better? What can you do to turn that *'No'* into a *'Yes'*? When should you next contact them? How do you continue to remain in touch? What can you do to get them more interested in your ideas?

Raising money for a project

There are two approaches to raising money:

◆ To ask for a donation towards the work of the organisation and its **general running costs**.

◆ To ask for support for some **specific piece of work** or a project or a programme that the organisation intends to undertake.

If you are simply seeking a general donation, you will stress the importance of the work that the organisation is doing, and that you need support to continue doing it. If you are raising money for a project, you will need to prepare a budget for that project, demonstrate the importance of the project, show how it fits within the overall objectives and work programme of the organisation, and then ask a prospective donor to support all or part of the project.

Why project fundraising is important

Most donors find it much more attractive to support a project than to make a contribution towards the costs of running the organisation. It gives them the feeling that they are paying for something specific that will be useful. They can see where their money is going, and that it will achieve results.

One important fundraising skill is to be able to think creatively about what sorts of projects to put forward. For example, if you are running a village library, then you might suggest the following as 'projects' for fundraising:

◆ Supporting the costs of the librarian, including any fee or honorarium being paid, costs of training and visits to the local town to buy books. The donor will feel that they are supporting a real person to run the library more effectively.

◆ Supporting the costs of buying books for the library for the next year. This would include the actual purchase costs of the books and also the travel and time taken in selecting and buying the books. The donor's money pays for books, and you can then show how the books will be read and used.

◆ Supporting a particular initiative, such as a health education programme. This could include the costs of purchasing a range of books on health matters plus the cost of organising discussions and training for village people on health maintenance. This would be of particular interest to someone interested in health matters. A gender programme could be organised for someone with that interest.

◆ Paying for a membership drive to increase the number of people using the library. This could include an event involving entertainment hosted by the library, a publicity drive in the village with songs and posters, and a number of free advice sessions on such topics as income-generation opportunities, health, consumer rights, where these subjects are explained through the contents of books that are available in the library.

◆ Paying for a literacy drive, where volunteers assist illiterate villagers to read and write.

Some of these items cover costs, which are already being incurred in the running of the library; others pay for additional items, which will help make the library more effective in its work. The budget for each project could also include a contribution to the general running costs of the library.

Thinking in project terms

An organisation has a budget as follows, which it is using as the basis for its fundraising:

Salaries	Rs	50,000
Rent, electricity, maintenance	Rs	10,000
Post, fax, phone	Rs	15,000
Transport; outstation and local	Rs	25,000
Sundry other costs	Rs	10,000
Total	**Rs**	**110,000**

Instead of presenting this as basic running costs, think about the expenditure in terms of the work it is supporting. You can present the same wonderful programme as follows:

Literacy/awareness project	Rs	40,000
Savings and Credit project	Rs	55,000
Tree nursery project	Rs	15,000
Total	**Rs**	**110,000**

You now have three projects to start fundraising for, each more interesting to the donor than supporting the organisation. All running costs (including staff salaries, the costs of running the office and transport) have been allocated within each project budget.

Some items will be more attractive than others to a particular donor. The fundraiser has to assess what is likely to appeal to the person they are about to approach for support alongside the organisation's own priorities for what it wants to do. The other factor is how much to ask for.

Costing a project

How you cost a project is important, as this determines how much you ask for—and how much you will get if your fundraising is successful. The starting point must be what the actual costs of doing the work are. You can calculate these in the following way:

Stage 1. Set out the actual expenditure you will incur in undertaking the work

◆ Write down all the items you are likely to incur expenses on.

◆ Estimate the cost of each item. You may need to do some research or to get a supplier to provide you with an estimate.

Stage 2. Allow for any 'hidden costs'

Many fundraisers forget to include certain costs, which will be incurred in running the project. Such things as:

◆ staff training;

◆ the purchase of publications or membership of a network;

◆ attendance at conferences;

◆ travel costs to meetings or to visit other projects to see what they are doing;

◆ an external evaluation; and

◆ producing a report of the project. And distributing it.

If you think that you are going to incur any of these expenses – or any other costs that you have forgotten to include – then include them in your budget.

Other costs that are often forgotten include services provided by the organisation to the project, such as:

◆ Office space—an allowance towards any rent being paid.

◆ Office services, such as electricity, cleaning and maintenance.

◆ Consumables, such as telephone and fascimile, photocopying, stationery, etc.

A reasonable estimate should be made for each of these and included in the budget.

Stage 3. Include the cost of staff time needed to implement the programme

Besides the things that you will have to pay for, there will be the costs of staff time that will be needed to do some work. If this is already being paid for from a larger grant towards your organisation's running costs, then you will not have to include this item in your budget as it is already being paid for. However, it is still useful to know the real cost of running the project.

Staff time can be calculated as follows for each member of staff who will be involved in the project:

◆ Estimate the number of days that will be required from each member of staff.

◆ Divide the monthly salaries of each member of staff plus the value of benefits by 15 to get the cost per day. This allows for public holidays, leave, time off owing to sickness, and attendance at meetings.

In your budget, you can either put the total figure for the cost of staff time, or show the number of days and the per diem cost for each person.

Stage 4. Include an allowance for the cost of running the organisation

Besides the cost of staff time, there is also the cost of running the organisation. This is the cost of the management time that is needed to supervise the project, and represents a contribution towards the cost of the Director and Board meetings. Again, these may be paid for out of a larger grant towards running costs, but you need this figure to be able to calculate the real cost of running the project.

If you are including this item in your budget, it can be called **Management and supervision costs**. You need to develop some sort of formula for calculating this cost, which you can justify. An usual range for such costs is 20–30% of staff costs.

Stage 5. Allow for inflation

For projects which will not be starting immediately or, which run over a period of time, you may need to make an allowance for inflation. If you include current costs, then when you come to pay the bills, you may find that the purchase price or salary levels have increased, and that there is not enough in the budget to pay the actual costs you have incurred.

How you allow for inflation, depends on present rates and forecasts. If the project is not due to start for some months or will run over more than one year, then include a reasonable estimate for inflation when calculating the cost of each item of expenditure.

Where you are applying for a grant to an overseas donor, you may need to calculate your budget and apply in a foreign currency (Euro, US$, £stg). You have to make a decision on the appropriate currency exchange rate to use. This should bear some relationship to current exchange rates, but you may need to be cautious in order to allow for possible adverse fluctuations in the exchange rate over the period of the grant. You want to reduce your exposure to currency risk, as this could mean that you did not have as much money as you had planned.

How much to ask for

Because of the way you calculate your costs, there is some flexibility in how much to ask for. You don't want to ask for more than you can spend. You don't want to ask for too little. You don't want to ask for more than the donor can afford. You need to bear in mind:

◆ the **real costs** of doing the work;

◆ how much you think the donor might be **prepared to contribute**; and

◆ the 'marketplace'—what **other organisations** are asking when fundraising for something similar.

What are your budget heads?

You are proposing to organise a training event for extension workers; these might be your budget heads:

• Cost of venue for one week.

• Cost of trainers to run the workshop.

• Per diem costs for extension workers to attend.

• Handouts and materials, including preparation time.

• Travel to and from venue.

• Preparation and supervision:

  Planning, promotion and briefing workshop leaders (1 person x 10 days).

  Attendance at venue by project staff (2 people x 5 days).

• Production of report:

  Writing and editing (1 person x 3 days).

  Typing and printing.

• Programme management (contribution towards organisation's costs).

• Sundry other costs and contingency (say 5% of total budget).

How much to ask for: A worked example

You are asking for sponsorship for a free weekly clinic at a hospital or health centre. Your budget includes:

- Direct programme expenditure; costs of doctors, nurses and staff on duty for the day, cost of medicines, and any promotion or publicity costs for the clinic: Rs 1,000 per day.
- A contribution towards the costs of running the building: Rs 800 per day.
- A contribution towards the costs of running the organisation: Rs 700 per day.

The total comes to Rs 2,500 for each day. How much do you ask for? You might consider the following:

- You may be trying to get support from individuals, and feel that they would be unlikely to contribute more than Rs 1,000. Based on your calculations, you know that this will cover the actuals (direct project costs), and you can find the other costs from your existing budget. You ask for Rs 1,000 to sponsor the clinic for one day. Or you could even divide the clinic into a morning and an afternoon session, and ask for Rs 1,000 to sponsor a session.
- You are approaching some leading companies in your town, and you feel that Rs 2,500 is too little to ask for. You might ask for Rs 10,000 to sponsor a clinic for one month.
- You are approaching a very large company. You might ask for Rs 125,000 to sponsor the weekly clinic for the next year. Or you could even suggest a donation of Rs 200,000, and include in your budget a healthy living campaign to encourage people to do something to improve their health (so that they will not need to come to the clinic).

The point is that how much you ask for is quite flexible, but it should be backed by a proper understanding of what the costs actually are.

Communicating the work of your organisation

Why communication is important

No fundraising can be done effectively without understanding the basic principles of communication. Promoting your organisation and its work is an important part of being successful in fundraising. People, therefore, talk of the importance of having a **communications and fundraising strategy**. Any publicity you get will:

◆ **Spread the message** about the need you are addressing and the importance of the work you are doing. Whether you are dealing with violence against women, helping refugees, addressing the consequences or causes of poverty, or promoting better education and health, it helps if more people know about why the need is important, as well as what you are doing about it. This creates a climate of understanding about the problem, that something needs to be done and that something can be done.

◆ **Enhance the reputation of your organisation**. When you approach people, if they have already heard good things about your organisation, it will be easier to persuade them to support you. They will have confidence that you can do a good job in addressing the problem or need, and that you will be able to spend their money effectively. This applies both to individuals as well as companies who might support you. It is also helpful when negotiating with government and donor agencies. Any good publicity you get also enhances the reputation of the voluntary sector as a whole.

◆ **Encourage people to come forward to support you**. This 'call to action' invites them to do something. If they feel strongly about the issue and want to help, they can give you money or offer to help in some way.

Getting publicity

Who is your publicity aimed at?

Any publicity is better than no publicity, but publicity will work best for you if:

◆   It is **targeted** at a particular group of people you want to reach.

◆   There is a **reason** (something you want to tell them or something you want them to do) for getting the publicity.

When thinking about who you want to reach, you should also think about how best you can reach them. You can reach decision-makers and professionals through features

---

CHECKLIST   Which of these are targets for your publicity?

These are some possible targets for your publicity. Which of these will you want to direct your publicity towards?

❑ Government at national level.

❑ Government at regional or state level.

❑ Government at district or local level.

❑ The local community in the areas that you work.

❑ Your beneficiaries or target groups.

❑ Community leaders.

❑ Other voluntary organisations.

❑ Key professionals, such as doctors, teachers, development workers.

❑ Opinion formers.

❑ The media.

❑ Business (to change business practice).

❑ The public at large (all-India, your state, your district, your city or town).

❑ Enquirers contacting you.

❑ Existing funders.

❑ Potential future funders.

❑ Existing members and supporters.

❑ Potential future members and supporters.

❑ The business sector as potential funders and supporters.

❑ Other *(please state)*:

in the national English language press. You can reach professionals through networks and associations, and the journals that they publish. You can reach voluntary sector professionals through magazines and journals produced for the voluntary sector (some are listed at the end of this book). You can reach business through the business press, and the more prestigious business journals. These are just some examples of how to reach your target audience.

Where to get publicity

There are all sorts of opportunities for publicising the work of your organisation. Think about the following:

◆ **National television and radio**. Which stations and what programmes?

◆ The **national newspapers**, including newspapers in regional languages.

◆ The **local press**, which can be particularly important for local organisations and when organising a local event.

◆ **Magazines**. There are a wide range of consumer interest and business magazines that might be interested in some aspect of your work.

◆ **Journals and newsletters**, including specialist voluntary sector publications; also those targeted at particular sections such as public administrators, health workers and teachers.

◆ **International media,** such as the newsletters of international organisations and donors, or journals devoted to development issues, such as *New Internationalist*.

There are many different ways of getting covered in a newspaper or magazine. These include:

◆ A **feature article** written by a professional journalist. Approach a newspaper and discuss the idea with a journalist who you know is interested in what you are doing, or ask a freelance journalist to write something and then try and get a newspaper to print it. If this is an in-depth feature, see if you can get a reply address printed at the end of the article, so that readers who are interested can write to you.

◆ A **news item**. Some news just happens, but sometimes you can make what you are doing 'newsworthy'. A natural disaster you are responding to is news. But, you may have just organised an important conference, and you will have to make this newsworthy. Even the winning of a major grant can be made into a news item. Some news is manufactured specially to get publicity, sometimes through some sort of 'stunt'. What are you doing that is newsworthy, or could be made to seem newsworthy? What could you do specially to attract publicity.

◆ A **photograph**. Sometimes, there is a good photo opportunity, which you can bring to the attention of the newspaper. Or you can provide them with suitable, good-quality pictures, which you have had taken. You should write a caption that explains what the photograph shows. This reinforces the message.

◆ A **quote within an article**. Many journalists have a list of 'experts' they refer to. They keep their names in their address book, and refer to this when some news breaks where they need information, advice or a response. Your aim is to become the person they approach in such circumstances. But make sure that they mention your organisation and get its name right!

◆ A **listing of an event or a service**. Some newspapers have lists of local services that are of interest to their readers. If you run a counselling service or give advice, get listed. If you are organising a craft fair or a fundraising event, the entertainments section of the paper might be interested in giving details.

◆ A **review of a publication**. Send review copies to all the magazines, newspapers and journals where you would like to get coverage. Enclose a press release that summarises the publication saying why it is interesting, as this makes it easy for a journalist to write a feature. Remember, though, that the publication must be of interest to the readers, if it is to get reviewed.

◆ A **letter to the editor**. Remember that only a short letter is likely to be printed. If you write to the newspaper on topics of concern to your organisation, you will begin to build a reputation as a leader in the particular field. You will also get replies from people interested in helping you.

◆ An **advertisement**. You will usually have to pay for this, but sometimes a newspaper might offer space free of cost, or you can find a well-wisher to pay the cost. The message in an advertisement is under your control—which is not so in a news item or feature written about you.

What to do

You need to be PR conscious, to understand the importance of publicity, and to be able to seek it wherever you can. This is not a matter of getting publicity for yourself; it is not an ego trip. You are trying to get noticed and attract support as part of your strategy for building a successful organisation. Here are some things you can do:

◆ Get to know **key journalists** on those newspapers and magazines which you are targeting for publicity.

◆ Whenever something happens that you feel should be covered, **prepare a press release** (together with photographs, where appropriate) and send this to the media you wish to cover the event. Telephone to see if it has been received and if they want more information.

◆ For really important events, organise a **press conference**.

◆ **Keep copies of every article** that is printed about your organisation, its work, and about the cause you are addressing. Keep these in a special file. Quote from

Some key components of effective communication

How to use the **AIDA principle** to create Attention, Interest, Desire and then Action.

Attention

- Creating a strong **brand image** for your organisation. This you will do through design (of your letterhead and publications) and through the publicity you get.

- A well-designed **logo**. And also a strapline that explains the work of your organisation clearly in a simple sentence. As an example, Karunashraya, a cancer hospice says 'There's no cure, but there's no limit to care'. Have you got a logo and a strapline? Are they modern or old-fashioned? Do they encapsulate what you're about?

- Some **simple slogans** that you can use to promote your work. Can you think of any?

- **Headlines** in all your communications (you can even use headlines in your fundraising applications to break up the text and draw attention to the different parts of the proposal).

- **Stunts** and events specially designed to draw attention to your organisation and its work.

Interest

- **Human stories** and **case studies**. You should be collecting these, and creating a dossier. They can illustrate the problem and the solution that you are providing in human terms.

- Using **photographs** (with captions) and illustrations. It's worth having good black and white photographs for use in your leaflets and reports, showing how you work with people. These should be well defined, with a good contrast and they should contain positive images of your work. A **video** can also be an important communications tool to create interest; but it should be short (five minutes is more than enough for most purposes).

- Using **facts and figures**, not talking in generalities (such as 'urgent problem' or 'desperate need'). These should be clipped from articles and reports and kept in a handy place until you need them. Some facts you will compile from your own researches.

- Using **charts and diagrams**, rather than unintelligible tables or figures. These can show the importance of a particular factor and also trends over time.

- **Explaining 'why'**, and not just saying 'what'.

Desire

- **Making a case**, creating a rationale for action. This is an important aspect of fundraising. You have to make people want to support you. You can do this by showing the importance and impact of what you are doing, and persuading people that they should support you in this.

- **Showing the impact** that an intervention can make—in human terms. What 'we' can do with 'your money'.

- Showing how other donors (companies and individuals) have been able to **make a difference**—and what it has meant to them. People feel secure if they know that others are doing the same thing.

- Using **endorsements** from prominent people, experts and users or beneficiaries. Again, this provides a 'comfort factor'.

these in reports about your work. Send photocopies of any article to key people; they may not have seen it, and it is a good excuse to write and to tell them something they did not know. Deepalaya, a Delhi-based organisation, used a collage of press-cuttings on its work as a cover design for one of its annual reports.

Remember that **not all media coverage is friendly**. Sometimes journalists are looking for 'dirt', which could interest their readers. Many journalists feel that voluntary organisations waste money or are corrupt; but this should not deter you. You want to get across the fact that the need or cause is important and that you are effective and honest. But you also need to know how to deal with bad publicity if and when it occurs.

Action

- Showing people that **they can do something**, and showing them what they can do. When you ask people to do something, be specific. Do not just say, 'You can help, if you are interested', rather 'If you would like to volunteer with us one evening a week, please telephone', or 'To sponsor an eye clinic each Wednesday costs just Rs 3,000; please help'.

- Providing a **response mechanism**, so that they can reply to you. This might be a reply address or a telephone number. You can set out what people can do and the response mechanism in a cut out panel with tick boxes and space for the respondent to fill in their name, address and phone (and e-mail) details.

The desired action might be:

- To contact you to show their interest.
- To give money or something else.
- To give their time as a volunteer.
- To offer a specialist skill.
- To do something to advance the cause in some way.
- To contact somebody else on your behalf.
- To recruit another supporter.
- To purchase something from you.
- To change their lifestyle in some way.

The Internet

Another facility to think about is a website. Here you can explain what you are doing and also mount an appeal for support. Voluntary organisations are now being encouraged to develop their own websites (the INDEV programme is being run through the British Council with World Bank support), and in a few years the Internet will be a common form of communication.

TO DO   Explaining your organisation

There are many occasions in fundraising when you need to explain the work of your organisation to people who know little or nothing about what you are doing. You need to catch their interest and keep their attention.

- Write down the **strapline** or slogan that your organisation uses (up to seven words).

If you don't have one, then make one.

- Write down the **Mission Statement** that has been agreed for your organisation.

If you don't have one, then write one in draft form (say, 50 words).

- Write down **five successes** that your organisation has achieved during the past year.

- And lastly, using all this information, in not more than 200 words, prepare **a written description of the work of your organisation,** which:

    - summarises your mission and key aims;

    - conveys the essence of what you are doing and the values underpinning your work; and

    - highlights the need for the organisation and the importance of its work.

TO DO   Asking for support

Prepare a five-minute talk (no longer), which is aimed at a group of Rotarians asking for support for your cause.

Remember the following:

- The audience is likely to **know nothing** about the work of your organisation.

- The audience is a group of business people from your city with an ethos of 'serving the community'. But they **know little about the field of social development**, and are certainly not used to jargon terms such as 'participatory rural appraisal'.

- You have to **capture their interest** by making the cause seem relevant to them, and by appealing to their emotions.

- Think about **the purpose of the presentation.** What do you want out of it? What do you want them to do? Is this realistic? Are they likely to respond?

- You don't have to use the whole of the five minutes. But don't over-run. Appeals that are too long make the listener 'switch off' and lose interest. **Short, sharp, lively and interesting**—that's what you should be aiming for.

- **Try out** (with a friend or into a tape recorder) **your talk before** you actually deliver it. Get as much feedback as possible. Make suggested improvements and then **go for it!**

EXERCISE What would you do if...

What would you do if...

You are invited to lunch with the editor of the main city newspaper.

Answer:

- Accept the invitation at once, and make sure you arrive five minutes early!

- Put together a background pack about the work of your organisation.

- Think about one or two interesting stories that the paper might cover, and prepare the main reasons why they might be of interest to readers.

- Think about a media campaign around the issue you are working on and whether the newspaper might be interested. Raise this idea at lunch to see if there is any interest.

- Listen. All sorts of things might come up in general conversation, which could indicate an interest that you can develop to help promote your organisation and its work.

What would you do if...

You have booked to attend a conference, where your organisation has some interesting ideas to contribute.

Answer:

- Make sure you have a badge that displays your name and organisation prominently, and that you have a good supply of business cards.

- Stand up and ask a question. Make sure it is a sensible question, which adds to the discussion. Announce your name and organisation prominently at the beginning.

- Look through the list of participants and speakers and see if there is anyone you need to meet. Make sure you meet them during lunch or coffee breaks.

- Bring along leaflets about the work of your organisation and leave them in a prominent position for people to take

- If the event is really important, ask if you can have a display or an information table or a book stall there.

- Make a note of anyone who seems really interested, and follow up a few days later with a letter and more information. You might even telephone one or two people you have met, to arrange an appointment.

What would you do if...

Someone turns up at your office and offers to fast to death for the cause.

Answer:

- Almost certainly, they are mad!

- But if you are convinced that they are genuine, that there is a real chance of organising a high profile campaign, then start talking...

Using case studies

Illustrating your work through a case study makes it easier for people to see the importance of what you are doing and helps you get their interest and support.

A case study can be based on a real life example, or it can be disguised to protect identity, or it might include facts from several examples in one 'composite' story, or it can be written hypothetically to reflect as honestly as possible what you are doing. Here are two examples:

Aziz is an orphan. Three years ago he was sold into slavery at age ten by his uncle. After two years, working 14 hours a day every day and scarcely ever seeing daylight, Aziz escaped and arrived on the streets of Bhopal to join the 10,000 other street children in the city. This was in 1996. We first came across Aziz when someone rang our 24-hour emergency helpline to tell us he had been beaten up and left for dead and was lying on the street. We were able to see him through hospital, paying all the bills. Since then we've kept in touch. Today Aziz works for us as a volunteer two evenings a week answering emergency calls from other street children, and we've also been able to help him with his ambition of becoming a carpenter. Each year at Child-Hope we answer over 8,000 calls, and we provide emergency assistance to over 1,000 street children, from providing medical assistance and dealing with problems with the police, to helping them make contact with their families and even returning them home, when they wish to do so and if it is possible. Child-Hope is a unique service helping some of our most vulnerable children at their time of greatest need, and giving them a future.

Fatima is a widow who lives in the hills of Andhra Pradesh. Life has been hard on her. She had a small plot of land to grow food to feed herself and her three children, but the crops often failed. She was in debt, and her position seemed hopeless. When we began work in her village, she made a decision to borrow a small sum of money through the credit scheme we were organising so that she could purchase two goats. These provided her with milk and some of this she was also able to sell and make some money. With this extra income she was now able to save, and quite soon she was able to repay the original loan. It wasn't long before she had saved enough to purchase a cow, and this further increased her income. Now she is paying for her youngest child to continue in school, and she hopes that he will soon get a seat in a technical college and then go on to get a qualification in forest management. Like you and me, Fatima has her own dreams and ambitions. With your help, we can make Fatima's dreams come true—and we can help others like her.

Both these stories show how the organisation works in order to change people's lives. This is far more powerful than simply talking about how you operate a telephone helpline service or a micro-credit scheme. It is your impact on people's lives that is important. And by including a case study, readers will be able to see that your work is successful and how it can change people's lives.

You can reinforce the point by giving the case study a 'catchy headline'. For example:

Creating hope for the street children of Bhopal

How we can turn a goat into a cow... and a cow into a qualification!

TO DO   Write a case study

Write a case study of how the work of your organisation has been able to make a difference, showing how there has been an impact on the life of an individual, family or community.

Producing simple and effective promotional materials

Promotional materials are important for communicating the work of the organisation and what it stands for. You will want to:

◆ Generate a **recognition and understanding** of your organisation, what it is doing and why its work is important.

◆ Promote a sense of **quality, leadership and innovation** in your field.

◆ Promote the **values** underpinning the work of the organisation.

If you are serious about fundraising, you will need a good (but not necessarily expensive) leaflet and an annual report or review of your work. These should be nicely written and attractively designed.

Types of promotional material

Many organisations do not have any printed material that promotes their work. Some do, but the material is poorly designed and written. An important first step in getting started in fundraising is to produce a range of promotional materials. We suggest four:

◆ A **simple leaflet** promoting your work. This will usually be a folded sheet of paper, perhaps four pages in an A5 format (or equivalent). This is cheap to produce and post. It is also long enough to contain all you need to say.

◆ A **series of fact sheets** about your main projects. Each might be one or two pages of A4, printed with text in two columns, and

Brochure – uninspiring

containing photographs and charts. This will provide people with all the information they need to know about a particular project, and can be handed out to visitors, taken to conferences and sent out on request.

Mobility India's Annual Report 1997–98; an appealing cover

◆ A larger **report of your work**. This often takes the form of an Annual Report. You have to produce annual accounts as a statutory reporting requirement. You should also be producing an annual review of your work as part of being transparent and accountable. The two can be combined into one document. Large voluntary organisations may be producing very substantial annual reports of 16 or even 32 pages. A smaller organisation might think in terms of a 4- or 8-page A4 report.

Alongside the accounts, the report will set out your achievements and your hopes for the future. It could contain case studies, the words of beneficiaries and experts, photographs, maps and explanatory diagrams and a lot more. This is an important publication, and you will want everyone who supports you to have a copy, and you will take it to meetings to hand out.

◆ A **newsletter** that can be sent out on a regular basis (perhaps half yearly at first). This helps keep people informed about the progress of your work. It also gives you an opportunity to ask them to support you (even if they have already given you a donation, they may respond to further requests for support). Your newsletter should be lively and interesting, not too long (4 pages of A4 is sufficient to start with), well illustrated with photographs and case studies, and show your organisation in a good light rather than deal with the problems and difficulties. Many newsletters fail because they are dull and poorly written, they concentrate on such things as conferences and meetings, rather than on the successes of the organisation and the human stories that can be found within its work.

If you are already producing a newsletter, then you can often improve it considerably with very little extra effort. One thing you can do is to show it to a professional journalist and a designer and ask for their comments. Another idea is to ask a few readers to tell you what they think. You can invite a few to a discussion or send out a short questionnaire. You may be surprised. You will also find that many of the people you are sending your newsletter to, throw it away without even reading it.

In each issue of your newsletter, you can feature a particular aspect of your work, and show how people can help you by giving financial support.

Getting information together

Once you have decided to produce some promotional material, you need to start collecting the information you will need for it. This might include some or all of the following:

◆ The **aims and mission** of the organisation. These should be clearly written and up-to-date. If you are producing a leaflet, this may be a good time to review your mission statement.

◆ A brief **history of the organisation**. This can include; why it was founded; the values of the organisation; its development from establishment to the present day; main achievements; some of the key people who have been involved since it started (you may need photographs of them). This information can usually be obtained from the organisation's files or from the founder.

◆ The **problem or need** being addressed, and its importance. You need to collect data that shows the problem, and also how things have been changing over time (getting better or worse!) and how the situation in your area compares with other states or regions in India and with other countries. This information can be gleaned from census data, research reports produced by international and Indian voluntary organisations and national institutes, policy documents produced by government and international agencies (such as the *Human Development Report,* published for the UNDP or *The State of the World's Children,* published by UNICEF). You may also be able to find useful policy statements to add to the data.

◆ The **processes and working methods** that your organisation is using in its work, and why they are special or innovative. This information is often contained in funding applications, but may need to be rewritten in understandable language. Think particularly about what is different and innovative about your approach, what is 'at the leading edge of social change', what is relevant to what others are doing and could be 'scaled up'.

◆ **Achievements and successes** of the organisation, including recent achievements. A useful exercise is to think of six achievements during the past year and six major achievements since the organisation was founded.

◆ **Case studies** of people helped. You may be able to get these from your records. Talk to as many people as possible and ask them to think of people and situations that can be used to illustrate the need, your work and your success. The case studies need not be lengthy. Fifty or 100 words is often sufficient, although you may want to write some in greater depth.

◆ **Endorsements and quotations** that enhance credibility of the organisation. Someone important may have written that, 'Your organisation is doing the most successful work in the field of...'. These quotations are extremely useful in emphasising how successful you are. They represent an expert or outside viewpoint, which is much more powerful than you saying how wonderful you are. If you have connections with prominent people, media personalities or experts, invite them to visit you. And then ask them to write to you commenting on what they have experienced. They will usually say something really nice. Then ask them if you can use this as a quote in your promotional literature.

◆ **Plans and aspirations**. Write a piece setting out the 'vision for the future' and some of the plans being developed.

◆ Where the **resources** come from and how they are spent? This is an important component of an annual report. You may want to include a simple pie chart for the organisation's income (broken down into its main sources), and another for expenditure. You may also want to show how the organisation has been growing over the past five or 10 years, which can be illustrated by growth in annual expenditure or numbers of people helped.

◆ A **call to action**. You want to use every opportunity to tell people that you need their support. You need to think about what you are going to ask people to do. It is often sensible to give several options, such as: make a donation; become a member; volunteer for an hour a week, etc. This 'call to action' can be included in a reply form with tick boxes that can be cut out and returned.

How to proceed

The following are the next things to do:

1. Develop some **clear objectives** (not more than three). Decide how you are going to distribute the publication and what you want it to achieve.

2. Produce **a synopsis** for your leaflet, identifying all the main areas of information to be included in the leaflet and the key points to be made in each section.

3. Decide **a format** for the leaflet and the approximate total number of words.

4. Do a **rough draft** for the text of the leaflet.

5. Make suggestions for **illustrations and photographs,** which could be used, and get together the illustrative material that you might use.

6. Do a **rough design** (a simple sketch showing all the pages and how the contents will be allocated to each page. Remember that simple, cheap printed material is

---

Some things to avoid in your leaflet

Many leaflets

- look **boring**; have no appeal; you don't feel like picking them up and reading them;

- **contain information of no interest**, such as the legal objectives or lists of supporters or a message from the Chairman that nobody is interested in;

- contain generalisations, information **not backed up by facts or examples**;

- are **difficult to read**, containing long chunks of text, not broken up, and with no headlines or sub-heads. If there are headlines, they are dull;

- use **long words and jargon** that the reader will not understand;

- have **no illustrations or photographs**;

- are extremely **poorly designed** and **badly printed**;

- are printed on **expensive paper** or thick card, which suggests a waste of resources;

- do not have clear **objectives**, and **no response is asked for**;

These are all things to avoid.

---

more cost-effective for smaller organisations. Large glossy brochures are expensive to produce and to post and give the impression of wasting money.

Further stages:

7. List **the audience** for the publication, and how they can be reached.

8. Draw up a **distribution plan**.

9. Decide a **print quantity**. This should relate to the distribution plan, but always print a few more copies 'just in case'. But don't make the mistake of printing too large a quantity, and then not know what to do with them once they are delivered to you by the printer.

Distributing a leaflet

The leaflet you produce will be your most important promotional tool. It can be used in a variety of ways to inform people and attract support:

◆ Send a copy to everyone on **your mailing list**.

◆ Give copies to all **members of staff to hand out** to people at meetings, conferences and to anyone else who is interested in your work.

◆ Have copies **in your office** to hand out to visitors.

The components of a successful leaflet

The following is a suggested structure for a four-page A5 format leaflet:

Page 1

- Your **name, logo and strapline** or brief statement explaining your **mission**.
- A **headline** with a **photograph** and about 30 words of **explanatio**n. This could be part of a story or theme that runs through the leaflet.

Page 2

- A brief **history** of the organisation (about 100 words, with a headline).
- A table showing four **key achievements**.
- A **quotation** from someone important.
- A **photograph** of the organisation at work with a **caption** (about six words).

Page 3

- A **case study** (about 50 words, with a headline).
- An **explanation of the need** with facts and figures or a chart (about 80 words, with a headline).
- A **photograp**h illustrating the case study with a caption (about six words).

Page 4

- Our **plans for the future** (about 60 words, with a headline).
- A **call to action**: how you can help (about 50 words with a headline).
- A **reply coupon** with tick boxes and room for the respondent to include name/address/phone number/e-mail address. This should include...
- A **reply address** for the respondent to reply to, and a telephone number for further information.

The leaflet should be well planned, and have a clear structure that takes the reader through from start to finish. It can have a theme running through (for example, 'Helping people to help themselves' or 'Making waves in Orissa').

The text needs to be well written and to the point. We have given some guidance on length; but even this could end up being too long. Write; then rewrite; then rewrite again until it is what you want.

Use headlines to signpost the different parts of the leaflet and emphasise the key points. Have a case study to show how you help people. Have several photographs with captions. A good photograph says more than many hundreds of words. The caption tells the reader what they are looking at.

Use tables to make information easily readable—as suggested above, while providing information on 'Our successes'. Diagrams and charts make figures easy to comprehend. Graphic techniques such as boxes can separate out the different components of the leaflet. If you are producing a leaflet, it is usually worthwhile getting a professional designer to help you.

◆ Send copies to **potential funders** that you have not yet approached with a short letter of introduction. If you have a good annual report, then you can send this as well.

◆ Enclose a copy with some of the **letters or packages** that are sent out from your office.

◆ Find ways of **reaching out to people** who might be interested in your work and in supporting you. This could include having a copy circulated with the newspaper in the area where your project is located; putting copies into people's letter boxes with a covering letter asking for support; finding a mailing list to circulate the leaflet to, possibly with an accompanying letter (such as the membership of the Bangalore Club), and starting a small direct mail fundraising campaign.

You should be able to use up at least 5,000 copies of your leaflet in this way. Think creatively about how you can get the leaflet circulated to more.

Managing donor relationships

Understanding the fundraising process

The task of a successful fundraiser is to:

◆ **identify potential donors**;

◆ **gain their interest** by telling them about your work; and

◆ **obtain their support**. Once they show interest, you can tell them what they can do to support you.

They can support you by making a donation, by becoming a member or a supporter of your organisation, by volunteering their time, or by signing a petition or getting involved in a campaign for change. Whatever they choose to do, it is because they are interested and want to do something. Your task then is to:

◆ **Thank them.**

◆ **Develop a relationship** with them so that they feel involved in the work of your organisation and can see that what they are doing (giving support, time) **is** making a difference.

◆ Get them to feel a sense of commitment to the cause and the work you are doing, so that they decide to give you **increased levels of support** and continue supporting you **over a long period**.

This all makes sense because:

◆ It is **difficult and expensive to find donors**, and fundraising only really makes sense if you can continue to get support from them. One measure that is often used is the 'lifetime value' of each donor; how much on average they will give during the period they are supporting you. If they continue to support you for many years, this can add up to a considerable amount.

◆ Your aim is to build a 'donor base' of committed supporters who will provide you with an assured, continuing and growing stream of income from year to year. This can include large numbers of smaller donors as well as smaller numbers of larger donors. It can include individuals a well as companies.

One term that is sometimes used in fundraising is 'friends for life'. Your aim in managing your donors is to make them just that.

Saying thank you

Once you have got their support, the next important step is to say thank you. You can do this by:

◆ **Writing** to them. Have a standard form of letter on your word processor, and personalise this when writing to them.

◆ **Telephoning** them. Here you can inject a sense of excitement, and begin to develop a relationship. This is certainly worth doing for all larger donations.

When thanking them, tell them:

◆ How **grateful** you are for their support.

◆ What it will be **spent on**, and what it will achieve.

◆ That you intend to **keep in touch**. This is where newsletters and annual reports can be used.

Many organisations forget to say thank you. This is a terrible mistake, as you will have a dissatisfied donor who will not want to continue giving. They will also tell other people how rude and ungrateful your organisation is. It is the job of the fundraiser not just to ask, but to say thank you whenever you are successful.

Building on a donor's interest

There are a number of ways of building on a donor's interest to create a greater sense of involvement and commitment. These include:

◆ **Reporting back** regularly and in some detail on what you have been able to do with the donor's money. You can do this by letter, by sending a newsletter, by sending them a copy of your annual report. Make sure that you have a procedure that ensures donors are kept informed regularly. This usually means creating a donor mailing list.

- Link their support to a **long-term programme** of development or support, and then tell them what you have been able to achieve with their money and report to them from time to time on the progress of the programme as a whole.

- Give the donor **information from the field**. Providing a field report, photographs or a video can all do this.

- **Link donor and beneficiary** in some way. For child sponsorship, the donor is linked to one particular child and receives reports about the progress of that child and the community as a whole. You may not want to do this, but you can provide case studies of success and feedback from beneficiaries and the communities you are helping with their money.

- Show how **the donor can do even more** to address the problem by building on the support that they have already given. Whenever you communicate, offer them opportunities to increase their support or give further support. But do this in a way that is friendly rather than aggressive. If they want to give more support, then you are giving them the opportunity to do so. One mistake that fundraisers often make is to assume that if somebody is giving, then they will not want to give in other ways.

- Take the donor into confidence by giving them **more information about the problem or need**. Keep them informed about continuing progress, emerging problems and needs and plans for the future. Show them how you (with their support) can do even more.

- Show them examples of **how other people have been able to help**. And for companies, how other companies have been able to help.

- Organise occasional **receptions and events** for donors. Donors can meet important people from the organisation and from public life. They can also meet each other. They can listen to an expert, meet and talk to beneficiaries or see a video that you have made.

- **Meet the donors** personally. Find out as much as you can about them and their reasons for giving. There may even be a personal connection with the problem. If you have a mailing list of 5,000 donors, obviously you can't meet all of them. But you can meet some of them, and this will give you some feedback about how they see your organisation, why they like supporting you, and what particularly interests them. Such 'market research' is invaluable in developing/sustaining a successful fundraising programme.

What makes a good fundraiser?

There are a number of important skills that you will need if you are to be successful. If you understand what skills are required, you can:

◆ **Assess your strengths,** and concentrate on doing those things you are good at.

◆ **Learn skills you need to acquire,** and set about obtaining necessary training or experience.

◆ **Find ways of compensating for your weaknesses** by mobilising others to help.

Key skills required

Here are some of the **key skills** required in a fundraiser:

• Commitment to the cause

You must really believe in the work that your organisation is doing and the need for it. Your enthusiasm and commitment will encourage others to become equally committed through their giving.

• The ability to ask

Many people feel uncomfortable actually asking for money or any other form of support. But you have to ask if you are to get anything, and the ability to ask is a key fundraising skill. Whether the task in hand is to write a four-page appeal letter, make a speech at a meeting of the Rotary Club, telephone a business to ask for a donation in kind, organise a committee to run a fundraising event, or pay a personal visit to seek the support of a major donor, all this requires an ability to ask effectively.

• Persuasiveness

People have choices as to what to do with their money. They have competing demands on what to spend it on. Your job is to persuade them that supporting your organisation is a really worthwhile 'investment' of their hard-earned money. You need to make a really good case and to present it in a persuasive way.

• Confidence and dealing with rejection

When you are asking for money, you need to radiate confidence. If you are apologetic or hesitant, people are much less likely to give to you. One of the biggest problems is maintaining your own confidence in the face of rejection. More people are likely to say 'No' than say 'Yes'—that is a fact of fundraising life—and it is very easy to get downhearted when things are not going too well. It is very important to pull youself together and approach the next prospective donor with equal enthusiasm, hope and commitment as you did the previous one.

• Persistence

Most fundraisers give up too soon. People often take 'No' to mean 'No'—rather than as a challenge to try to convert the 'No' into a 'Yes'. If you give up there is no chance at all. If you feel that they really should be supporting you, then you should try to find another way of persuading them and try to get them to change their mind.

• Truthfulness

The fundraiser has to be truthful at all times. The need to persuade people can create pressure to tell partial truths and to claim more for your work than is the case. You must be truthful about the work of your organisation, its success and the impact of the work. Present your work in 'good light', but do not exaggerate or distort facts.

• Social skills

A good fundraiser needs confidence and patience. A confident appeal is harder to refuse. Patience in dealing with the concerns of donors is very important. A good fundraiser should also like meeting and dealing with people, should remember names and faces (and even personal details) and be chatty and cheerful.

• Contacts and the ability to make contacts

The fundraiser who already has a number of existing contacts in an area or sector (such as business) will be at an enormous advantage. But having contacts does not necessarily mean that these will be the people who will want to support the organisation. A good alternative is to have the confidence to ask anybody for what is needed, the ability to make new contacts and the good sense to ask others to do the asking for you.

• Imagination and creativity

The task may be to dream up new activities that will inspire existing supporters and to create events that the public is going to be enthused by. Or to present your work in an exciting and imaginative way. Circumstances are continually changing and new opportunities emerging, so fundraisers need to identify new approaches and not simply rely on what has been done in the past.

• Opportunism

You need to grasp every opportunity that presents itself. For example, if a leading company has just announced a major hike in profits or has been awarded a major construction contract in your area, then a cleverly constructed appeal for funds might just succeed. If there is a feature in the newspaper focusing on your cause, then a request at the end of the article with a reply address or a letter to your existing supporters with a photocopy of the article are both likely to bring in support. The annual calendar provides opportunities at different times of the year, for example Diwali, Eid and the New Year provide extremely good fundraising opportunities.

• Organisational skills

Good organisation is essential. Fundraisers have to keep voluminous files of correspondence and information on donation history for each donor. All this must be organised so that no past event or piece of generosity is forgotten.

• An ability to recognise weaknesses

Nobody is perfect. You are unlikely to fulfil all the criteria needed for successful fundraising. A good fundraiser is able to recognise his or her weaknesses, and to do something about them. There are several things you can do:

Concentrate on doing the things you are good at. If you're terrified about chatting up millionaires and prefer to write letters or organise fundraising events, do that.

Find others to help you, who are good at some aspect of fundraising. There may be someone who is terrific on the telephone, who you could use to ring around companies asking for support in kind.

Learn from experience, and do things better next time.

Get trained, if there are relevant and good opportunities for training.

Set up a support group, a small fundraising committee to take an interest in what you are doing, to advise you and to help out when there's just too much for you to do.

And finally...

Many people find the idea of fundraising frightening. They dislike asking. They do not know who to ask or even how to set about fundraising. They feel that donors will not give. They are embarrassed about the whole thing. As a result, they either do not bother to do any fundraising, or they are not very good at it.

A good fundraiser understands the fundraising process and why people want to give, understands why the money is needed and that it will be used to do something important, understands that they have to ask before they will get, and is enthusiastic enough to want to find and persuade people to support the work of the organisation.

Think about the following:

◆ What are your **fears** about fundraising?

◆ What do you see as **barriers** to being successful?

Read the book again—more carefully this time—because the answers are all here! Fundraising should not be frightening. Fundraising is vital, as otherwise your organisation will not have enough money to do its work. It is also a privilege to be able to offer donors an opportunity to do good and to have their money used for something that they will be proud of.

Useful contacts

Books for Change
28 Castle Street, Ashoknagar, Bangalore   560 025
Tel   080-5098240, 5549556   Fax   080-5586284
E-mail   bfcbgl@satyam.net.in   Website   www.booksforchange.com
Contact   Shobha Ramachandran

Charities Aid Foundation (CAF)
25 Navjeevan Vihar, New Delhi   110 017
Tel   011-6522206   Fax   011-6186646
E-mail   cafindia@vsnl.com
Contact   Mathew Cherian

Centre for Advancement of Philanthropy (CAP)
Mulla House (Jehangir Wadia Building) 4th Floor
51 M.G. Road, Flora Fountain, Mumbai   400 001
Tel   022-2675397   Fax   022-2675642
E-mail   centphil@bom7.vsnl.net.in
Contact   Noshir Dadrawala

Indian Centre for Philanthropy (ICP)
Sector C, Pocket 8/8704, Vasant Kunj, New Delhi   110 070
Tel   011-6897659   Fax   011-6121917
E-mail   icp@vsnl.com
Contact   Pushpa Sundar

Murray Culshaw Advisory Services (mcas)
139/4 Domlur Layout, Domlur, Bangalore   560 071
Tel   080-5543770, 5560003
E-mail   murray@vsnl.com
Contact   Murray Culshaw

National Foundation for India (NFI)
PO Box 3133, Indian Habitat Centre, Zone 4-A
Upper Ground Floor, Lodhi Road, New Delhi   110 003
Tel   011-4641864/65   Fax   011-4641867
E-mail   sghose@nfi.ren.nic.in
Contact   Shankar Ghose, Director

The Other India Bookstore
Above Mapusa Clinic, Mapusa, Goa   403 507
Tel   0832-263505
Contact   Claude and Norma Alvares

Partners in Change
S–136 Greater Kailash, Part II, New Delhi   110 048
Tel   011-6483595
E-mail   pic@actionaidindia.org
Contact   Shankar Venkateswaran

Rashtriya Gramin Vikas Nidhi (RGVN)
Kannachal, Silpukuri, Guwahati   781 003, Assam
Tel   0361-544725   Fax   0361-521980
E-mail   rgvn@gw1.vsnl.net.in
Contact   Prabhab Dutta

South Asian Fund Raising Group (SAFRG)
A–97, Defence Colony, Ground Floor
New Delhi   110 024
Tel   011-2160210
E-mail   safrg@del3.vsnl.net.in
Contact   Rajeev Dua, Executive Secretary

United Way of Vadodara
C/o The Federation of Gujarat Industries, R.C. Dutt Road
Vadodara 390 005, Gujarat
Tel   0265-328091   Fax   0265-339298
Contact Girdhar Vaswani

Voluntary Agencies Network India (VANI)
H–17/1 Malviya Nagar, New Delhi   110 017
Tel   011-6854899
E-mail   vani@nda.vsnl.net.in
Contact   Anil Singh, Executive Secretary

Index of subjects

Index of organisations

About the authors

Michael Norton is Director of the Centre for Innovation in Voluntary Action (CIVA), a UK-based NGO. CIVA has a number of Indian programmes including: Books for Change, which it founded as a specialist publisher for the development sector; Books for All, which is a village publishing programme in Andhra Pradesh; and the NFI Innovations Fund, which is a partnership with the National Foundation for India and Oxfam to make grants for social innovation. Michael Norton also runs communications workshops for NGOs, mainly in Hyderabad through the Centre for Development Communication. He is author the of *The WorldWide Fundraiser's Handbook*, published in the UK for the International Fund Raising Group.

Michael Norton, CIVA, 9 Mansfield Place
London NW3 1HS

Tel 0044-171-4311412 Fax 0044-171-4313739
E-mail norton@civa.prestel.co.uk

Murray Culshaw was formerly Director of Oxfam in India and now runs Murray Culshaw Advisory Services (mcas), a Bangalore-based consultancy group specialising in fundraising research, consultancy and training. He has helped several voluntary organisations to get started with communications and fundraising. He started a payroll scheme for Charities Aid Foundation in Bangalore, which has now been extended to Delhi. Murray Culshaw has previously edited *PROFILE 300*, which provides information on 300 selected voluntary organisations and networks in India. He is one of the promoters *of BangaloreCares,* which develops business and public support for voluntary organisations in Karnataka. Currently he is undertaking research into the public accountability and reporting of voluntary organisations.

Murray Culshaw, mcas, 139/4 Domlur Layout, Domlur, Bangalore 560 071

Tel 0091-80-5543770, 5560003
E-mail murray@vsnl.com

New from Sage

Evaluating Development Aid

Issues, Problems and Solutions

Basil Cracknell

This book is a clear, balanced and comprehensive guide to the subject of evaluating development aid. Broadly divided into two parts, the first half reviews the basic issues of evaluating aid—objectives, methodology, the difference between monitoring and evaluation, and feedback. Throughout, special emphasis is placed on the logical framework approach. The need to focus on outcomes rather than on outputs is also highlighted.

In the second part of the book, Basil Cracknell shifts the focus from the role of the donor to the role of the recipient. The topics discussed include the importance of evaluating impact and sustainability; stakeholder analysis, problems particular to various sectors including research and development; poverty alleviation and structural adjustment; international cooperation; the participatory approach; and 'Fourth Generation Evaluation'.

The recurring theme of this very lucid and authoritative book is the central dilemma facing aid evaluators today; how to reconcile the requirements of objectivity and accountability with the realisation that some form of participation is essential to properly understand the impact of people-centred projects on the intended beneficiaries.

Written by a very experienced aid evaluator and supported by examples from actual evaluations, this practical hands-on book will be of interest to all aid and donor agencies; consultants; professionals and academics in the fields of development studies, economics and management; voluntary agencies at the grassroots; government agencies in the field of development; and aid evaluators.

CONTENTS: *List of Figures/List of Boxes/List of Acronyms and Abbreviations/Foreword* by Robert Chambers/*Acknowledgements*/Introduction/**Part 1** A Brief History of Aid Evaluation/**Part 2** Basic Issues: Purposes, Techniques and Methods/**Part 3** Monitoring, Learning and Feedback/**Part 4** Impact, Empowerment, Stakeholder Analysis and the Participatory Approach/**Part 5** The Wider Horizon and the Way Ahead/*References/Index/About the Author*

220mm × 140mm/387pp/Hb/Pb/Rs 495/Rs 250/2000

Sage Publications
New Delhi/Thousand Oaks/London

of related interest

Organisations and Development
Strategies, Structures and Processes

Reidar Dale

The theme of this book is organisation analysis pertaining to societal development. Reidar Dale explores the concept of development bringing terms and ideas from the academic fields of development studies, planning, public administration and management. Among the topics covered are: the types and forms of development organisations; formulating strategies for development work; modes of development planning; people's participation in development work; organisation and institution building; and evaluation of development work.

The author provides innovative perspectives and interpretations on several topics, including, a typology of development organisations, perspectives on strategy formulation, a typology of organisational forms in the development field, coordination mechanisms relating to development work, and a basic evaluation model.

Lucidly written and supported by illustrations, this book is a must for all those in the field of development.

CONTENTS: *List of Figures, Tables and Boxes/Foreword* by Hands Detlef Kommeier/*Preface/* 1. Conceptualising Development/2. Organisations in Development/3. Strategy Formulation for Development/4. Organisational Features and Work Categories/5. Participation, Empowerment and Capacity-Building/6. Evaluating Development Organisations and Their Work/*References/Index/About the Author*

220mm × 180mm/Hb/Pb/Rs 395/Rs 225/2000

Sage Publications
New Delhi/Thousand Oaks/London